THE NINJA AIR FRYER COOKBOOK UK XXL

Super-Delicious & Amazing Air Fryer Recipes for Everyday Enjoyment I incl. Breakfast, Lunch, Dinner, Desserts & More I Nutritional Facts I International Dishes

MARGARETE MILLER

© 2024 Margarete Miller

All rights reserved

All rights for this book here presented belong exclusively to the author.

Usage or reproduction of the text is forbidden and requires a clear consent of the author in case of expectations.

ISBN – 9798326807397

TABLE OF CONTENTS

Introduction 8
    Getting Started with Your Ninja Air Fryer 10
    Tips for optimal air frying 13
    Ingredient Guides 16
        Essential Ingredients 16
        Substitutions and Variations 21

Chapter 1: North America 27

United States 28
    Buffalo Wings 29
    Southern Fried Chicken 30
    Mac and Cheese Bites 31
    Apple Pie 32

Canada 33
    Poutine 34
    Maple-Glazed Carrots 35
    Butter Tarts 36
    Nanaimo Bars 37

Mexico 38
    Taquitos 39
    Carne Asada Tacos 40
    Mexican Street Corn 41
    Churros 42

Chapter 2: South America 43

Brazil 44
    Coxinha (Chicken Croquettes) 45
    Feijoada (Black Bean Stew) 47
    Pão de Queijo (Cheese Bread) 48
    Brigadeiros 49

Argentina 50
    Empanadas 51
    Asado (Grilled Beef) 53
    Chimichurri Potatoes 54
    Alfajores 55

Peru 56
    Ceviche Tostadas 57
    Lomo Saltado 58
    Peruvian Corn 59
    Picarones (Pumpkin Donuts) 60

Chapter 3: Europe 61

Italy 62
    Bruschetta 63
    Chicken Parmesan 64
    Garlic Bread 65
    Tiramisu Bites 66

France 68
    Escargot 69
    Coq au Vin 70
    Ratatouille 71
    Crème Brûlée 72

Spain 73
    Patatas Bravas 74

 Paella 75
 Gambas al Ajillo (Garlic Shrimp) 76
 Flan 77

Germany 78
 Pretzels 79
 Schnitzel 80
 Sauerkraut Balls 81
 Black Forest Cake 82

United Kingdom 83
 Scotch Eggs 84
 Fish and Chips 85
 Roast Potatoes 86
 Sticky Toffee Pudding 87

Chapter 4: Asia 88

China 89
 Spring Rolls 90
 Sweet and Sour Chicken 91
 Fried Rice 93
 Sesame Balls 94

Japan 95
 Gyoza 96
 Teriyaki Salmon 97
 Tempura Vegetables 98
 Mochi 99

India 100
 Samosas 101
 Butter Chicken 102
 Naan Bread 104
 Gulab Jamun 105

Thailand 106
    Satay Skewers 107
    Pad Thai 109
    Thai Basil Vegetables 110
    Mango Sticky Rice 111

Chapter 5: Middle East 112

Lebanon 113
    Falafel 114
    Shawarma 115
    Hummus and Pita Chips 116
    Baklava 117

Turkey 118
    Sigara Borek (Cheese Rolls) 119
    Doner Kebab 120
    Bulgur Pilaf 121
    Lokma (Sweet Fried Dough) 122

Conclusion 123

Disclaimer 124

INTRODUCTION

This is your gateway to a culinary adventure that spans continents and cultures, all from the comfort of your own kitchen. This cookbook is for anyone who enjoys exploring new flavours and cooking techniques, while enjoying the convenience and health benefits of air frying. Whether you're an experienced cook or just starting out, this book offers a delightful blend of simplicity, innovation and global cuisine.

The Ninja Air Fryer has revolutionised the way we cook, offering a healthier alternative to traditional frying without compromising on taste and texture. Using rapid air circulation technology, the Ninja Air Fryer cooks food evenly and quickly, using little or no oil. This means you can enjoy crispy, delicious meals that are lower in fat and calories. The versatility of the Ninja Air Fryer allows you to fry, bake, roast and reheat, making it a multi-functional tool in your kitchen arsenal.

In this cookbook, we take you on a culinary journey through different continents and countries, showcasing the rich and varied flavours of the world. Each chapter is dedicated to a specific country and offers a curated selection of four recipes, including a starter or snack, main course, side dish and dessert. These recipes have been carefully adapted to be prepared in the Ninja Air Fryer, so you can enjoy traditional dishes with a modern, healthier twist.

As you flip through the pages of this cookbook, you'll be transported to the bustling markets of the Middle East, the vibrant street food scenes of Asia, the hearty cuisines of Europe, and the comfort food havens of North and South America. Each chapter focuses on a specific country, offering a curated selection of four recipes: an appetiser or snack, a main course, a side dish, and a dessert. All the recipes have been adapted to be cooked in an air fryer, ensuring healthier versions of your favourite dishes without compromising on taste and texture.

To make your cooking experience seamless, each recipe in this book is structured to provide clear and detailed instructions. Here's what you can expect from every recipe:

- **Name**: The title of the recipe.
- **Short Description**: A brief overview with interesting facts about the dish.
- **Key Points:**

Serves: The number of portions the recipe makes.
Difficulty: The skill level required (Easy, Moderate, or Difficult).
Prep Time: The time needed to prepare the ingredients.
Cook Time: The time needed to cook the dish.
Total Time: The total time required to make the recipe.

- **Ingredient List**: A detailed list of all the ingredients you will need.
- **Preparation:** Step-by-step instructions to guide you through the cooking process.
- **Tip**: A useful tip to enhance your cooking experience or the dish's flavour.
- **Estimated Nutritional Table per 100g:** Nutritional information to help you keep track of your dietary intake.

Each recipe is marked with a symbol that indicates the type of dish. These symbols help you quickly identify the kind of recipe you are looking at. Here's what the symbols mean:

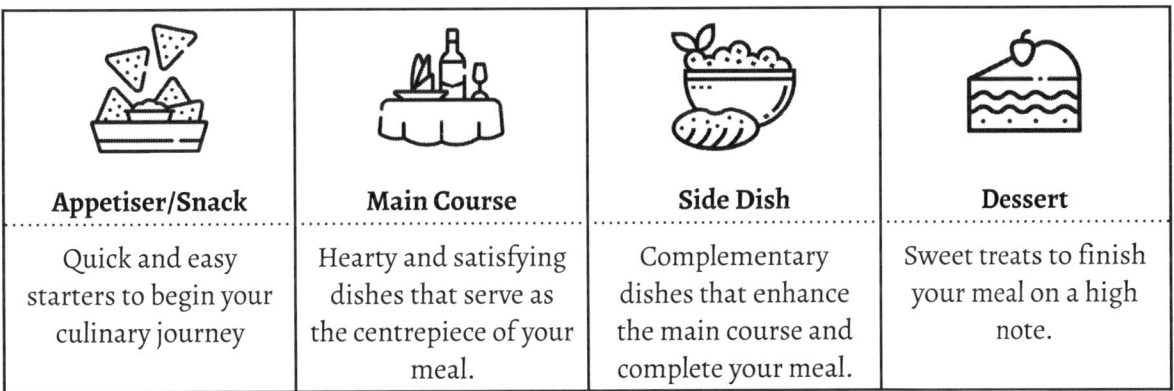

Appetiser/Snack	Main Course	Side Dish	Dessert
Quick and easy starters to begin your culinary journey	Hearty and satisfying dishes that serve as the centrepiece of your meal.	Complementary dishes that enhance the main course and complete your meal.	Sweet treats to finish your meal on a high note.

We invite you to join us on this culinary adventure and discover new flavours and cooking techniques from the comfort of your own kitchen. With the Ninja Air Fryer, you can create delicious and healthy meals that reflect the rich culinary heritage of different countries.

Happy cooking and bon appétit!

Getting Started with Your Ninja Air Fryer

Choosing the right kitchen appliance can make all the difference in your cooking experience, and the Ninja Air Fryer stands out as a versatile, efficient, and health-conscious option. The Ninja Air Fryer is not just a trendy gadget; it is a revolutionary tool that transforms how we approach everyday cooking. Here's a comprehensive look at why the Ninja Air Fryer should be your go-to appliance and the numerous benefits of air frying.

Versatility and Multifunctionality

One of the most compelling reasons to choose the Ninja Air Fryer is its versatility. This appliance is designed to perform multiple cooking functions, including air frying, roasting, baking, reheating, and dehydrating. Whether you want to prepare crispy chicken wings, roast vegetables, bake a cake, or dehydrate fruits for a healthy snack, the Ninja Air Fryer can handle it all. This multifunctionality means you can replace several kitchen appliances with just one, saving you space and reducing clutter.

Health Benefits of Air Frying

The primary appeal of air frying is its health benefits. Traditional frying methods require submerging food in oil, which significantly increases the fat and calorie content of your meals. In contrast, the Ninja Air Fryer uses rapid air circulation to cook food, requiring little to no oil. This method reduces the fat content by up to 75% compared to traditional frying, making it an excellent option for those looking to eat healthier without sacrificing taste. Air frying also helps retain the nutritional value of the ingredients. Since the cooking process is faster and requires minimal oil, vitamins and minerals in the food are better preserved. This is particularly important for vegetables, which can lose significant nutrients when overcooked or deep-fried.

Superior Cooking Performance

The Ninja Air Fryer is engineered with advanced technology to ensure superior cooking performance. Its rapid air circulation system cooks food evenly and quickly, resulting in a crispy exterior and tender interior. This ensures that your food is perfectly cooked every time, with a texture and flavour that rivals traditional frying methods. The appliance's wide temperature range (typically from 40°C to 200°C) allows you to cook a variety of dishes with precision. The Ninja Air Fryer also features multiple cooking presets, making it easy to achieve optimal results for different types of food without guessing.

Convenience and Ease of Use

Another significant advantage of the Ninja Air Fryer is its convenience. The appliance is user-friendly, with intuitive controls and digital displays that make it easy to set cooking times and temperatures. Many models come with pre-programmed settings for common foods, so you can start cooking with the touch of a button.

Cleaning up after cooking is also a breeze. The Ninja Air Fryer's components, such as the basket and crisper plate, are typically non-stick and dishwasher safe. This means you can spend less time scrubbing and more time enjoying your meals.

Energy Efficiency

Air fryers, including the Ninja Air Fryer, are generally more energy-efficient than conventional ovens. They preheat quickly and cook food faster, which reduces overall energy consumption. This not only saves you time but also lowers your electricity bills. In addition, the compact size of the air fryer means it generates less heat, making it a cooler and more comfortable appliance to use, especially in warmer months.

Safety Features

Safety is a top priority in kitchen appliances, and the Ninja Air Fryer excels in this area. It is equipped with various safety features, including automatic shut-off, cool-touch handles, and non-slip feet. These features ensure that you can cook with confidence, knowing that the appliance will not overheat and that it is stable on your countertop.

Environmental Impact

Using less oil and energy not only benefits your health and wallet but also has a positive impact on the environment. The reduction in oil usage means fewer resources are required for cooking, and the energy efficiency of the Ninja Air Fryer contributes to a smaller carbon footprint. Choosing an air fryer is a step towards more sustainable cooking practices.

Culinary Creativity

The Ninja Air Fryer opens up a world of culinary creativity. With its ability to perform various cooking functions, you can experiment with different recipes and techniques. The appliance encourages you to try new dishes from around the world, making your cooking experience more exciting and diverse. From crispy Korean fried chicken to delicate French pastries, the Ninja Air Fryer allows you to explore global cuisines with ease.

Consistent Results

One of the challenges in cooking is achieving consistent results, especially with complex dishes. The Ninja Air Fryer's precise temperature control and even heat distribution ensure that your food is cooked uniformly every time. This reliability means you can replicate your favourite recipes with confidence, knowing that they will turn out perfectly each time.

Ideal for Busy Lifestyles

For those with busy lifestyles, the Ninja Air Fryer is a game-changer. Its quick cooking times mean you can prepare meals in a fraction of the time it would take using traditional methods. This is particularly beneficial for weeknight dinners when time is limited. The ability to cook directly from frozen means you can go from freezer to table in minutes, making it easier to stick to a healthy eating plan even on hectic days.

Perfect for Small Spaces

The compact design of the Ninja Air Fryer makes it ideal for small kitchens, dorm rooms, or RVs. Despite its smaller footprint, it offers ample cooking capacity, allowing you to prepare meals for the whole family without taking up too much counter space.

Community and Support

Ninja Air Fryer users benefit from a vibrant community of enthusiasts who share recipes, tips, and tricks. Online forums, social media groups, and dedicated websites offer a wealth of resources to help you get the most out of your air fryer. This sense of community and the availability of support make the Ninja Air Fryer an even more valuable addition to your kitchen.

In a nutshell: The Ninja Air Fryer is a versatile, efficient and health-conscious choice for anyone looking to improve their cooking experience. Its ability to produce delicious, crispy food with minimal oil, combined with its user-friendly features and energy efficiency, makes it a standout appliance in any kitchen. Choosing a Ninja air fryer is an investment in a healthier lifestyle, greater convenience and endless culinary possibilities. Enjoy the journey of exploring global flavours with the confidence and ease that the Ninja Air Fryer brings to your culinary adventures.

Tips for optimal air frying

Using an air fryer can transform your cooking experience, making it easier to prepare healthier, delicious meals with minimal effort. To help you get the most out of your Ninja Air Fryer, here are some detailed tips for optimal air frying, complete with specific examples:

1. Preheat Your Air Fryer

Just like an oven, preheating your air fryer before adding your food can make a big difference in the cooking process. Preheating ensures that the air fryer reaches the desired cooking temperature, leading to more even and consistent cooking. Most air fryers only need about 3-5 minutes to preheat. For example, preheat the air fryer to 200°C (390°F) when making chicken wings to ensure they cook evenly and get that perfect crispy skin.

2. Don't Overcrowd the Basket

For the best results, avoid overcrowding the air fryer basket. Leaving space between food items allows hot air to circulate more effectively, resulting in evenly cooked and crispy dishes. If you need to cook a large batch, consider doing it in multiple smaller batches. For instance, when making French fries, cook them in a single layer and shake the basket halfway through cooking for best results.

3. Shake or Turn Foods Halfway Through Cooking

To ensure even cooking and browning, shake the basket or turn food items halfway through the cooking time. This is especially important for foods like fries, chicken wings, and vegetables. For example, if you're cooking breaded fish fillets, turning them halfway through ensures both sides are crispy and golden brown.

4. Use a Light Coating of Oil

While air frying significantly reduces the amount of oil needed compared to traditional frying, using a small amount of oil can help achieve a crispy texture. Lightly coat your food with oil using a spray bottle or brush. Avoid using aerosol sprays directly on the air fryer basket, as they can damage the non-stick coating. For example, spray a light coat of olive oil on sweet potato fries to enhance their crispiness.

5. Pat Foods Dry Before Cooking

Moisture can prevent food from crisping up properly. Pat foods dry with a paper towel before air frying, especially if you're cooking something that has been marinated or thawed from frozen. Removing excess moisture ensures a better texture. For instance, pat dry chicken pieces after marinating to ensure a crispy exterior.

6. Experiment with Cooking Times and Temperatures

Different foods require different cooking times and temperatures. While the Ninja Air Fryer comes with presets, don't be afraid to experiment to find the optimal settings for your favourite recipes. Keep a record of what works best for each type of food. For example, if you find that your homemade onion rings are too dark at the recommended temperature, try lowering the temperature and increasing the cook time slightly.

7. Use Parchment Paper or Silicone Mats

Using parchment paper or silicone mats can prevent food from sticking to the basket and make cleanup easier. Make sure to use air fryer-specific parchment paper with holes to allow proper air circulation. Avoid covering the entire basket, as this can hinder airflow. For example, use a perforated parchment paper when baking cookies in the air fryer to prevent sticking and ensure even cooking.

8. Season Food Properly

Season your food generously before air frying to enhance the flavours. Since air frying can sometimes strip away moisture, robust seasoning helps maintain the taste. Experiment with different spices and herbs to find your perfect flavour combinations. For example, season potato wedges with rosemary, garlic powder, and paprika for a tasty side dish.

9. Clean Your Air Fryer Regularly

Regular cleaning is essential to keep your air fryer in top condition and prevent lingering flavours from transferring to different dishes. Clean the basket, tray, and interior of the air fryer after each use. Most parts are dishwasher safe, but always refer to the manufacturer's instructions. For example, if you cook fish, clean the basket immediately afterward to prevent any residual fishy smell from affecting your next dish.

10. Use the Right Accessories

Using the right accessories can expand the capabilities of your air fryer. Accessories like grill racks, skewers, and baking pans designed for air fryers can help you cook a wider variety of dishes. Make sure any accessory you use fits well and allows for proper air circulation. For instance, use an air fryer-compatible cake pan to bake a small cake or a batch of brownies.

11. Avoid Cooking Foods with High Water Content

Foods with high water content, like fresh tomatoes or watery vegetables, may not crisp up as well in the air fryer. Consider draining or patting dry such foods before cooking, or opt for other cooking methods to achieve the desired texture. For example, if you want to cook zucchini, slice it, pat it dry, and coat it with a light layer of breadcrumbs to help achieve a crispy exterior.

12. Reheat Leftovers

The air fryer is excellent for reheating leftovers, giving them a crisp texture that microwaves often fail to achieve. To reheat, set the air fryer to a lower temperature (about 150°C/300°F) and cook until the food is heated through, usually for 5-10 minutes. For example, reheat leftover pizza slices in the air fryer to revive their crispy crust.

13. Use a Meat Thermometer

For meats, using a meat thermometer ensures that they are cooked to the proper internal temperature, providing both safety and optimal taste. This is especially important for thicker cuts of meat. For instance, ensure that chicken breasts reach an internal temperature of 75°C (165°F) before serving.

14. Adjust for Altitude and Climate

Cooking times and temperatures might vary slightly depending on your altitude and climate. Higher altitudes might require longer cooking times, while more humid environments might need adjustments to achieve the desired crispiness. For example, if you live in a high-altitude area, check your food a few minutes before the recommended cooking time and adjust accordingly.

15. Rest Cooked Foods

Allow cooked foods to rest for a few minutes after air frying. This helps redistribute the juices, especially in meats, making them more succulent and flavourful. For example, let air-fried steak rest for 5 minutes before slicing to retain its juices.

By following these detailed tips, you can make the most out of your Ninja Air Fryer and enjoy delicious, healthy meals with minimal hassle. Air frying offers a unique combination of convenience, health benefits, and versatility, making it a valuable addition to any kitchen. Happy air frying!

Ingredient Guides

Essential Ingredients

Stocking your pantry with the right ingredients is crucial for making the most out of your Ninja Air Fryer. Here is a guide to the essential ingredients you'll need to create delicious and diverse air-fried meals from this cookbook.

Oils

While air frying requires significantly less oil than traditional frying methods, having a variety of oils on hand can enhance the flavour and texture of your dishes.

- **Olive Oil:** Ideal for Mediterranean dishes and a healthy option for most cooking.
- **Vegetable Oil:** A neutral oil suitable for a wide range of recipes.
- **Sesame Oil:** Adds a distinct flavour to Asian dishes.
- **Coconut Oil:** Great for baking and adds a unique taste to certain recipes.
- **Avocado Oil:** High smoke point makes it perfect for high-temperature air frying.

Flours and Breading

Creating that perfect crispy texture often requires some type of flour or breading.

- **Plain Flour:** Essential for breading and battering.
- **Cornflour:** Great for making light, crispy coatings.
- **Breadcrumbs:** Used for a crunchy coating on meats, vegetables, and more.
- **Panko Breadcrumbs:** Provide an extra-crispy texture, especially popular in Japanese cuisine.

Almond Flour: A gluten-free alternative that works well for breading.

Seasonings and Spices

A well-stocked spice rack can transform simple ingredients into flavourful dishes.

- **Salt and Pepper:** Basic seasonings for enhancing flavour.
- **Paprika (Sweet and Smoked):** Adds colour and a depth of flavour.
- **Cumin:** Essential for Middle Eastern and Mexican dishes.
- **Coriander:** Used in a variety of global cuisines for its citrusy flavour.
- **Turmeric:** Adds colour and a subtle earthiness.
- **Garlic Powder:** Convenient for adding garlic flavour without the mess.

- → **Onion Powder:** Adds a sweet, oniony flavour.
- → **Chilli Powder:** Brings heat and complexity to your dishes.
- → **Oregano:** A staple in Italian and Greek cooking.
- → **Thyme and Rosemary:** Essential for Mediterranean dishes.
- → **Cinnamon:** Used in both sweet and savoury dishes, particularly Middle Eastern cuisine.

Sauces and Condiments

These are indispensable for marinades, dressings, and finishing touches.

- → **Soy Sauce:** A key ingredient in Asian cooking.
- → **Fish Sauce:** Adds depth and umami to Thai and Vietnamese dishes.
- → **Worcestershire Sauce:** Great for adding a savoury kick.
- → **Hot Sauce:** For adding heat to any dish.
- → **Tahini:** Essential for Middle Eastern dishes like hummus.
- → **Mustard:** Useful in marinades and sauces.
- → **Mayonnaise:** Perfect for creating dips and spreads.
- → **Ketchup:** A common condiment and a base for various sauces.

Grains and Legumes

These pantry staples form the basis of many side dishes and mains.

- → **Rice (Jasmine, Basmati, Arborio):** Essential for a variety of global cuisines.
- → **Quinoa:** A healthy, protein-rich grain.
- → **Couscous and Bulgur Wheat:** Key ingredients in Middle Eastern dishes.
- → **Chickpeas:** Used in many Mediterranean and Middle Eastern recipes.
- → **Lentils:** Versatile and nutritious, perfect for soups and stews.

Dairy and Non-Dairy Alternatives

Keep these on hand for a variety of recipes.

- → **Milk (Dairy or Plant-Based):** Used in batters, sauces, and baking.
- → **Butter:** Adds richness and flavour to many dishes.
- → **Yoghurt:** Essential for marinades and sauces, especially in Middle Eastern and Indian cuisines.
- → **Cheese (Feta, Parmesan, Cheddar):** Adds flavour and texture.

Fresh Produce

While fresh produce should be bought as needed, there are some staples you might always want to have on hand.

- → **Garlic and Onions:** Base flavours for many dishes.
- → **Lemons and Limes:** Essential for adding acidity and brightness.
- → **Fresh Herbs (Parsley, Coriander, Mint, Basil):** Add fresh, vibrant flavours.
- → **Tomatoes:** Used in sauces, salads, and more.
- → **Bell Peppers:** Versatile and add sweetness and colour.
- → **Leafy Greens (Spinach, Kale):** Great for adding nutrition and texture.

By keeping these essential ingredients stocked, you'll be prepared to tackle any recipe in the Ninja Air Fryer Cookbook. These staples form the foundation of diverse, delicious meals from around the world, ensuring you can always whip up something tasty with ease. But choosing the right produce and proteins is also essential for achieving the best results with your air fryer. Here's a comprehensive guide to help you select the best ingredients for air frying, ensuring your dishes are always delicious and perfectly cooked.

Produce

Vegetables

Potatoes and Root Vegetables

- → **Best Varieties:** Russet potatoes, sweet potatoes, carrots, parsnips, and beets.
- → **Selection Tips:** Choose firm, unblemished vegetables. Avoid any with sprouts or green spots, as these can be bitter.
- → **Air Frying Tips:** Cut into even-sized pieces for uniform cooking. Lightly coat with oil and season before air frying.

Cruciferous Vegetables

- → **Best Varieties:** Broccoli, cauliflower, Brussels sprouts.
- → **Selection Tips:** Look for bright green, tightly packed florets for broccoli and cauliflower. Choose Brussels sprouts that are firm and free of yellowing leaves.
- → **Air Frying Tips:** Cut into bite-sized pieces. Lightly coat with oil and season. Shake the basket halfway through cooking for even browning.

Peppers and Tomatoes

- → **Best Varieties:** Bell peppers, cherry tomatoes, grape tomatoes.
- → **Selection Tips:** Choose peppers with smooth, shiny skin and tomatoes that are firm and free of blemishes.
- → **Air Frying Tips:** For peppers, slice into strips or chunks. For tomatoes, keep whole or halved. Lightly coat with oil and season.

Leafy Greens

- → **Best Varieties:** Kale, spinach, Swiss chard.
- → **Selection** Tips: Look for vibrant, crisp leaves. Avoid any with wilting or yellowing.
- → **Air Frying Tips:** For kale chips, remove the stems and tear leaves into bite-sized pieces. Lightly coat with oil and season.

Mushrooms

- → **Best Varieties:** Button mushrooms, cremini mushrooms, portobello mushrooms.
- → **Selection Tips:** Choose mushrooms that are firm and free of slimy spots. Clean with a damp cloth rather than washing to avoid water absorption.
- → **Air Frying Tips:** Slice evenly. Lightly coat with oil and season. Mushrooms cook quickly, so monitor closely.

Fruits

Firm Fruits

- → **Best Varieties:** Apples, pears, pineapples.
- → **Selection Tips:** Choose fruits that are firm and free of bruises or soft spots.

Air Frying Tips: Slice into even pieces. Lightly coat with a sprinkle of cinnamon and a touch of oil or honey.

Stone Fruits

- → **Best Varieties:** Peaches, nectarines, plums.
- → **Selection Tips:** Look for fruits that are slightly firm but yield to gentle pressure.
- → **Air Frying Tips:** Halve and remove the pit. Lightly coat with oil or a drizzle of honey.

Proteins

Meat

Chicken

- → **Best Cuts:** Chicken breasts, thighs, drumsticks, wings.
- → **Selection Tips:** Choose organic or free-range chicken for the best flavour. Look for pink flesh without any grey or green discolouration.
- → **Air Frying Tips:** Marinate or season well before cooking. For even cooking, ensure pieces are of similar size. Preheat the air fryer for crispy skin.

Beef

- → **Best Cuts:** Ribeye steak, sirloin steak, ground beef for patties.
- → **Selection Tips:** Look for well-marbled cuts for juiciness and flavour. Choose grass-fed beef for better quality.
- → **Air Frying Tips:** Season steaks generously and allow them to come to room temperature before air frying. For burgers, form patties evenly and avoid pressing down during cooking.

Pork

- → **Best Cuts:** Pork chops, tenderloin, ribs.
- → **Selection Tips:** Choose pork that is pale pink with a small amount of fat marbling. Avoid cuts with dark spots or excessive liquid in the packaging.
- → **Air Frying Tips:** Brine pork chops for added moisture. Season well and cook at a moderate temperature to avoid drying out.

Seafood

Fish

- → **Best Varieties:** Salmon, cod, tilapia.
- → **Selection Tips:** Look for firm, moist fillets with a fresh sea smell. Avoid fish with a strong odour or dull flesh.
- → **Air Frying Tips:** Pat fish dry before seasoning. Use a light coat of oil to prevent sticking. Cook skin-side down for fillets with skin.

Shellfish

- → **Best Varieties:** Shrimp, scallops.
- → **Selection Tips:** Choose shrimp with firm, translucent flesh. For scallops, look for a creamy white colour and firm texture.

- → **Air Frying Tips:** Marinate shrimp for added flavour. Pat dry before cooking. Scallops should be dry-packed for best results.

Plant-Based Proteins

Tofu
- → **Best Varieties:** Extra-firm tofu.
- → **Selection Tips:** Choose tofu that is firm and free of excess liquid.
- → **Air Frying Tips:** Press tofu to remove excess moisture. Marinate or season well. Cut into even-sized cubes or slices.

Tempeh
- → **Selection Tips:** Choose tempeh that is fresh and free of dark spots or strong odour.
- → **Air Frying Tips:** Steam tempeh before marinating to reduce bitterness. Cut into strips or cubes for even cooking.

Seitan
- → **Selection Tips:** Look for fresh, refrigerated seitan. Ensure it is firm and free of off smells.
- → **Air Frying Tips:** Marinate or season well. Slice into even pieces for consistent cooking.

Additional Tips for Selecting Produce and Proteins
- → **Seasonality:** Choose produce that is in season for the freshest flavour and best quality. Seasonal fruits and vegetables are often more affordable and taste better.
- → **Local and Organic:** When possible, choose local and organic produce and proteins. They are often fresher and free from pesticides and hormones.
- → **Storage:** Properly store your produce and proteins to maintain their freshness. For example, store root vegetables in a cool, dark place and keep meats in the coldest part of your refrigerator.

By selecting the best produce and proteins, you can ensure that your air-fried dishes are not only healthy, but also bursting with flavour.

Substitutions and Variations

Cooking with an air fryer opens up a world of possibilities, and being able to substitute ingredients or vary recipes to suit dietary needs, preferences, or availability can enhance your culinary creativity. Here are some useful substitutions and variations to help you adapt recipes to your taste or dietary requirements.

Dairy Substitutions

Milk
- → **Substitute with:** Almond milk, soy milk, coconut milk, oat milk.
- → **Use in:** Baking, batters, sauces.
- → **Tip:** Unsweetened versions are best for savoury dishes to avoid altering the taste.

Butter
- → **Substitute with:** Coconut oil, olive oil, vegan butter.
- → **Use in:** Baking, frying, roasting.
- → **Tip:** For baking, solid fats like coconut oil work best. For roasting or frying, olive oil or vegan butter can be used.

Cheese
- → **Substitute with:** Nutritional yeast, vegan cheese.
- → **Use in:** Toppings, fillings, sauces.
- → **Tip:** Nutritional yeast can add a cheesy flavour without the dairy. Vegan cheeses are great for melting.

Egg Substitutions

Eggs in Baking
- → **Substitute with:** Flaxseed meal (1 tbsp flaxseed meal + 3 tbsp water = 1 egg), chia seeds (1 tbsp chia seeds + 3 tbsp water = 1 egg), applesauce (1/4 cup = 1 egg).
- → **Use in:** Cakes, muffins, pancakes.
- → **Tip:** These substitutes work well as binders and provide moisture.

Eggs for Coating
- → **Substitute with:** Plant-based milk with a little flour, aquafaba (the liquid from a can of chickpeas).
- → **Use in:** Breading, battering.
- → **Tip:** Aquafaba is excellent for creating a sticky coating to adhere breadcrumbs or flour.

Meat Substitutions

Chicken
- → **Substitute with:** Tofu, tempeh, seitan, jackfruit.
- → **Use in:** Stir-fries, curries, grilling.

- → **Tip:** Marinate tofu or tempeh to infuse them with flavour. Jackfruit works well in shredded chicken recipes.

Beef
- → **Substitute with:** Mushrooms, lentils, plant-based meat substitutes.
- → **Use in:** Stews, tacos, burgers.
- → **Tip:** Mushrooms and lentils provide a hearty texture similar to beef. Plant-based meats are great for a direct substitute in most recipes.

Fish
- → **Substitute with:** Tofu, tempeh, heart of palm.
- → **Use in:** Fish sticks, fillets, seafood stews.
- → **Tip:** Marinate tofu or tempeh with seaweed flakes or dulse to impart a seafood flavour. Heart of the palm can mimic the texture of fish in recipes.

Gluten-Free Substitutions

Flour
- → **Substitute with:** Almond flour, coconut flour, gluten-free all-purpose flour, rice flour.
- → **Use in:** Baking, breading, thickening.
- → **Tip:** Gluten-free flours can behave differently, so it's often best to use recipes specifically designed for them or add a binding agent like xanthan gum.

Breadcrumbs
- → **Substitute with:** Crushed gluten-free crackers, ground nuts, gluten-free panko.
- → **Use in:** Breading, toppings.
- → **Tip:** Ground nuts add extra flavour and crunch, making them a great alternative to traditional breadcrumbs.

Grain Substitutions

Rice
- → **Substitute with:** Quinoa, cauliflower rice, bulgur wheat (for non-gluten-free).
- → **Use in:** Side dishes, stir-fries, salads.
- → **Tip:** Quinoa provides a protein boost, while cauliflower rice is a low-carb option.

Pasta
- → **Substitute with:** Zucchini noodles (zoodles), spaghetti squash, gluten-free pasta.

- → **Use in:** Pasta dishes, salads, casseroles.
- → **Tip:** Zoodles and spaghetti squash are great low-carb options. Gluten-free pasta is widely available and works well as a direct substitute.

Vegetable Substitutions

Potatoes
- → **Substitute with:** Sweet potatoes, parsnips, turnips.
- → **Use in:** Fries, mashes, roasts.
- → **Tip:** Sweet potatoes add a different flavour profile and more nutrients. Parsnips and turnips offer unique flavours and textures.

Bell Peppers
- → **Substitute with:** Zucchini, eggplant, mushrooms.
- → **Use in:** Stir-fries, stuffing, grilling.
- → **Tip:** Zucchini and eggplant provide similar textures, while mushrooms add a different, but complementary, flavour.

Sweetener Substitutions

Sugar
- → **Substitute with:** Honey, maple syrup, agave nectar, coconut sugar.
- → **Use in:** Baking, sauces, marinades.
- → **Tip:** Liquid sweeteners like honey and maple syrup can add moisture to recipes, so you may need to adjust other liquid ingredients accordingly.

Honey
- → **Substitute with:** Agave nectar, maple syrup, date syrup.
- → **Use in:** Baking, dressings, marinades.
- → **Tip:** These substitutes have similar consistencies and sweetness levels, making them easy swaps.

Customizing Recipes for Special Diets

Vegan Variations
- → **Replace dairy with plant-based alternatives** like almond milk, soy yoghurt, and vegan cheese.
- → **Use flaxseed or chia seed eggs** in place of regular eggs in baking.

- → **Substitute meat with plant-based proteins** like tofu, tempeh, seitan, and legumes.

Low-Carb Variations

- → **Use cauliflower rice or zucchini noodles** instead of regular rice or pasta.
- → **Replace potatoes with turnips or cauliflower** in mashes and roasts.
- → **Opt for low-carb sweeteners** like stevia or erythritol instead of sugar.

Allergen-Friendly Variations

- → **Use nut-free butters** like sunflower seed butter if you have a nut allergy.
- → **Opt for gluten-free flours and grains** to accommodate gluten sensitivities.
- → **Choose soy-free plant-based proteins** like pea protein or hemp seeds if you have a soy allergy.

Now that we've explored the essential ingredients and discussed possible substitutions and variations, it's time to dive into the heart of this cookbook – the recipes!

We hope this collection of global flavours inspires you to get creative in the kitchen.

Happy cooking, bon appétit, and happy air frying!

EXCLUSIVE BONUS

40 Weight Loss Recipes

&

14 Days Meal Plan

Scan the QR-Code and receive the FREE download:

CHAPTER 1: NORTH AMERICA

UNITED STATES

BUFFALO WINGS

Buffalo Wings are a popular American appetiser known for their spicy, tangy flavour. Traditionally deep-fried, this air fryer version provides a healthier alternative without sacrificing the crispy texture and bold taste.

Serves: 4 | Difficulty: Easy | Prep Time: 10 minutes | Cook Time: 25 minutes | Total Time: 35 minutes

INGREDIENT LIST:

- 1 kg chicken wings, split and tips removed
- 1 tbsp vegetable oil
- 1 tsp salt
- 1/2 tsp black pepper
- 1/2 tsp garlic powder
- 1/2 tsp paprika
- 60ml hot sauce (such as Frank's RedHot)
- 50g unsalted butter, melted
- Celery sticks and blue cheese dressing, to serve

PREPARATION:

1. **Season the Wings:** In a large bowl, toss the chicken wings with vegetable oil, salt, black pepper, garlic powder, and paprika until evenly coated.
2. **Air Fry the Wings:** Preheat the air fryer to 200 °C (390 °F). Arrange the wings in a single layer in the air fryer basket. Cook for 25 minutes, shaking the basket halfway through, until the wings are golden and crispy.
3. **Prepare the Buffalo Sauce:** In a small saucepan over low heat, combine the hot sauce and melted butter. Stir until well combined and heated through.
4. **Coat the Wings:** Place the cooked wings in a large bowl. Pour the Buffalo sauce over the wings and toss until they are well coated.
5. **Serve:** Transfer the wings to a serving platter and serve immediately with celery sticks and blue cheese dressing on the side.

Tip: For an extra kick, add a pinch of cayenne pepper to the Buffalo sauce. Ensure the wings are in a single layer in the air fryer to allow for even cooking and maximum crispiness.

ESTIMATED NUTRITIONAL TABLE PER 100G:

Calories: approx 220 kcal | Fat: approx 15 g | Carbohydrates: approx 1 g | Fibre: approx 0 g | Protein: approx 20 g | Salt: approx 1.2 g

SOUTHERN FRIED CHICKEN

Southern Fried Chicken is an iconic American dish known for its crispy, flavourful coating and juicy, tender meat. This air fryer version delivers all the deliciousness with less oil and a quicker cooking time.

Serves: 4 | Difficulty: Moderate | Prep Time: 15 minutes | Cook Time: 25 minutes | Total Time: 40 minutes

INGREDIENT LIST:

- 4 chicken thighs, bone-in and skin-on
- 4 chicken drumsticks
- 250ml buttermilk
- 1 tsp hot sauce (optional)
- 200g plain flour
- 1 tsp paprika
- 1 tsp garlic powder
- 1 tsp onion powder
- 1/2 tsp cayenne pepper
- 1/2 tsp salt
- 1/2 tsp black pepper
- 2 tbsp vegetable oil

PREPARATION:

1. **Marinate the Chicken:** In a large bowl, combine the buttermilk and hot sauce. Add the chicken thighs and drumsticks, ensuring they are fully coated. Cover and refrigerate for at least 1 hour or overnight for best results.
2. **Prepare the Coating:** In another bowl, mix the plain flour, paprika, garlic powder, onion powder, cayenne pepper, salt, and black pepper.
3. **Coat the Chicken:** Remove the chicken pieces from the buttermilk, allowing any excess to drip off. Dredge each piece in the seasoned flour mixture, pressing firmly to ensure an even coating.
4. **Preheat the Air Fryer:** Preheat the air fryer to 180 °C (360 °F). Lightly brush or spray the chicken pieces with vegetable oil.
5. **Air Fry the Chicken:** Place the chicken in the air fryer basket in a single layer. Cook for 25 minutes, turning halfway through, until the coating is golden brown and crispy, and the chicken is cooked through (the internal temperature should reach 75 °C).
6. **Serve:** Let the chicken rest for a few minutes before serving to allow the juices to redistribute. Serve hot.

Tip: For an extra crispy coating, double dip the chicken by repeating the buttermilk and flour coating process before air frying. Serve with coleslaw and mashed potatoes for a classic Southern meal.

ESTIMATED NUTRITIONAL TABLE PER 100G:

Calories: approx 240 kcal | Fat: approx 14 g | Carbohydrates: approx 10 g | Fibre: approx 1 g | Protein: approx 18 g | Salt: approx 0.7 g

MAC AND CHEESE BITES

Mac and Cheese Bites are a delightful twist on the classic comfort food, offering crispy, bite-sized portions perfect for snacking or as an appetiser. This air fryer version ensures a crunchy exterior with a gooey, cheesy centre.

Serves: 4 | Difficulty: Moderate | Prep Time: 20 minutes (plus chilling time) | Cook Time: 12 minutes | Total Time: 32 minutes (plus chilling time)

INGREDIENT LIST:

- 200g macaroni
- 1 tbsp butter
- 1 tbsp plain flour
- 250ml whole milk
- 200g grated cheddar cheese
- 50g grated parmesan cheese
- Salt and pepper, to taste
- 2 large eggs, beaten
- 100g plain flour
- 150g breadcrumbs
- Cooking spray

PREPARATION:

1. **Cook the Macaroni:** Cook the macaroni according to the package instructions until al dente. Drain and set aside.
2. **Make the Cheese Sauce:** In a saucepan, melt the butter over medium heat. Stir in the flour and cook for 1 minute. Gradually add the milk, whisking continuously until the sauce thickens. Remove from heat and stir in the cheddar and parmesan cheeses until melted. Season with salt and pepper.
3. **Combine and Chill:** Mix the cooked macaroni with the cheese sauce until well combined. Spread the mixture into a baking dish and refrigerate for at least 1 hour or until firm.
4. **Form the Bites:** Once the mac and cheese mixture is firm, cut it into bite-sized squares or use a spoon to form small balls.
5. **Coat the Bites:** Place the flour, beaten eggs, and breadcrumbs into separate bowls. Dredge each mac and cheese bite in flour, then dip in the beaten eggs, and finally coat with breadcrumbs. Press gently to ensure the breadcrumbs adhere.
6. **Preheat the Air Fryer:** Preheat the air fryer to 200 °C (390 °F).
7. **Air Fry the Bites:** Lightly spray the coated bites with cooking spray. Place them in the air fryer basket in a single layer. Cook for 10-12 minutes, turning halfway through, until golden and crispy.
8. **Serve:** Allow the bites to cool slightly before serving. Enjoy hot.

Tip: For an extra flavour boost, add a pinch of cayenne pepper or smoked paprika to the cheese sauce. Serve with a side of marinara sauce for dipping.

ESTIMATED NUTRITIONAL TABLE PER 100G:
Calories: approx 270 kcal | Fat: approx 15 g | Carbohydrates: approx 22 g | Fibre: approx 1 g | Protein: approx 10 g | Salt: approx 0.8 g

APPLE PIE

Apple Pie is a classic American dessert featuring sweet, spiced apple filling encased in a buttery, flaky crust. This air fryer version allows for a quick and easy way to enjoy this beloved treat with a perfectly crisp finish.

Serves: 4 | Difficulty: Moderate | Prep Time: 20 minutes | Cook Time: 25 minutes | Total Time: 45 minutes

INGREDIENT LIST:

For the Crust:
- 250g plain flour
- 125g cold unsalted butter, cubed
- 1 tbsp caster sugar
- 1/2 tsp salt
- 3-4 tbsp cold water

For the Filling:
- 3 medium apples (such as Bramley or Granny Smith), peeled, cored, and sliced
- 50g light brown sugar
- 1 tsp ground cinnamon
- 1/4 tsp ground nutmeg
- 1 tbsp lemon juice
- 1 tbsp plain flour

For Assembly:
- 1 egg, beaten (for egg wash)
- 1 tbsp demerara sugar (optional)

PREPARATION:

1. **Make the Crust:** In a large bowl, combine the flour, caster sugar, and salt. Add the cold butter and rub it into the flour mixture with your fingertips until it resembles coarse crumbs. Gradually add the cold water, one tablespoon at a time, and mix until the dough comes together. Form the dough into a ball, wrap it in cling film, and refrigerate for at least 30 minutes.
2. **Prepare the Filling:** In a bowl, combine the sliced apples, light brown sugar, ground cinnamon, ground nutmeg, lemon juice, and plain flour. Mix well and set aside.
3. **Roll out the Dough:** On a lightly floured surface, roll out half of the dough to fit the base and sides of your air fryer-safe pie dish. Place the rolled dough into the dish, pressing it into the edges.
4. **Add the Filling:** Spoon the apple filling into the pie crust, spreading it out evenly.
5. **Top the Pie:** Roll out the remaining dough to cover the top of the pie. Place it over the apple filling and crimp the edges to seal. Cut a few slits in the top crust to allow steam to escape. Brush the top with beaten egg and sprinkle with demerara sugar if desired.
6. **Preheat the Air Fryer:** Preheat the air fryer to 180 °C (360 °F).
7. **Air Fry the Pie:** Place the pie dish in the air fryer basket. Cook for 20-25 minutes, or until the crust is golden brown and the filling is bubbly.
8. **Serve:** Allow the pie to cool slightly before slicing. Serve warm, optionally with vanilla ice cream or custard.

Tip: For a decorative touch, use cookie cutters to cut shapes out of the top crust before placing it on the pie. This also helps the steam escape and adds a beautiful presentation.

ESTIMATED NUTRITIONAL TABLE PER 100G:
Calories: approx 220 kcal | Fat: approx 10 g | Carbohydrates: approx 32 g | Fibre: approx 2 g | Protein: approx 2 g | Salt: approx 0.2 g

CANADA

POUTINE

Poutine is a Canadian classic that combines crispy chips, rich gravy, and melted cheese curds. This air fryer version ensures the chips are perfectly golden and crisp, providing the ideal base for this indulgent dish.

Serves: 4 | Difficulty: Moderate | Prep Time: 15 minutes | Cook Time: 30 minutes | Total Time: 45 minutes

INGREDIENT LIST:

- 4 large potatoes, peeled and cut into chips
- 2 tbsp vegetable oil
- Salt, to taste
- 250ml beef or chicken gravy
- 200g cheese curds

PREPARATION:

1. **Prepare the Chips:** Soak the cut potatoes in cold water for 30 minutes to remove excess starch. Drain and pat dry with a clean tea towel.
2. **Season and Cook the Chips:** Preheat the air fryer to 180 °C (360 °F). Toss the potatoes with vegetable oil and a pinch of salt. Place the chips in the air fryer basket in a single layer. Cook for 25-30 minutes, shaking the basket halfway through, until golden and crispy. Remove and keep warm.
3. **Heat the Gravy:** While the chips are cooking, heat the gravy in a saucepan over medium heat until it reaches a simmer.
4. **Assemble the Poutine:** Place the hot chips on a serving platter. Sprinkle the cheese curds evenly over the top. Pour the hot gravy over the chips and cheese curds, allowing the cheese to melt slightly.
5. **Serve:** Serve immediately while the chips are hot and the cheese curds are melty.

Tip: For extra flavour, season the chips with a pinch of garlic powder or paprika before air frying. You can also add additional toppings such as pulled pork or sautéed mushrooms for a gourmet twist.

ESTIMATED NUTRITIONAL TABLE PER 100G:

Calories: approx 200 kcal | Fat: approx 10 g | Carbohydrates: approx 20 g | Fibre: approx 2 g | Protein: approx 7 g | Salt: approx 1.0 g

MAPLE-GLAZED CARROTS

Maple-Glazed Carrots are a delightful side dish that highlights the natural sweetness of carrots with a rich maple syrup glaze. This air fryer version ensures perfectly caramelised carrots with a hint of savoury flavour.

Serves: 4 | Difficulty: Easy | Prep Time: 10 minutes | Cook Time: 15 minutes | Total Time: 25 minutes

INGREDIENT LIST:

- 500g carrots, peeled and cut into sticks
- 2 tbsp olive oil
- 3 tbsp maple syrup
- 1/2 tsp salt
- 1/4 tsp black pepper
- 1 tsp fresh thyme leaves (optional)

PREPARATION:

1. **Prepare the Carrots:** In a large bowl, toss the carrot sticks with olive oil, maple syrup, salt, black pepper, and fresh thyme leaves if using.
2. **Preheat the Air Fryer:** Preheat the air fryer to 200 °C (390 °F).
3. **Air Fry the Carrots:** Place the carrots in the air fryer basket in a single layer. Cook for 12-15 minutes, shaking the basket halfway through, until the carrots are tender and caramelised.
4. **Serve:** Transfer the maple-glazed carrots to a serving dish and serve immediately.

Tip: For a touch of spice, add a pinch of cayenne pepper or smoked paprika to the carrots before air frying. Garnish with a sprinkle of fresh parsley for an extra burst of colour and flavour.

ESTIMATED NUTRITIONAL TABLE PER 100G:
Calories: approx 70 kcal | Fat: approx 3 g | Carbohydrates: approx 10 g | Fibre: approx 2 g | Protein: approx 1 g | Salt: approx 0.4 g

BUTTER TARTS

Butter Tarts are a classic Canadian dessert, featuring a flaky pastry shell filled with a rich, gooey mixture of butter, sugar, and eggs. This air fryer version makes it easy to enjoy these sweet treats with a perfectly crisp crust.

Serves: 12 | Difficulty: Moderate | Prep Time: 20 minutes | Cook Time: 15 minutes | Total Time: 35 minutes

INGREDIENT LIST:

For the Pastry:
- 250g plain flour
- 1/2 tsp salt
- 170g cold unsalted butter, cubed
- 4-5 tbsp ice water

For the Filling:
- 120g dark brown sugar
- 120g golden syrup
- 60g unsalted butter, melted
- 1 large egg
- 1 tsp vanilla extract
- 1/4 tsp salt
- 50g raisins or chopped pecans (optional)

PREPARATION:

1. **Make the Pastry:** In a large bowl, mix the plain flour and salt. Cut in the cold butter until the mixture resembles coarse crumbs. Add ice water, one tablespoon at a time, until the dough comes together. Form the dough into a ball, wrap in cling film, and refrigerate for at least 30 minutes.
2. **Prepare the Filling:** In a medium bowl, whisk together the dark brown sugar, golden syrup, melted butter, egg, vanilla extract, and salt until smooth. Stir in the raisins or chopped pecans if using.
3. **Preheat the Air Fryer:** Preheat the air fryer to 180 °C (360 °F).
4. **Assemble the Tarts:** Roll out the pastry on a floured surface to about 3mm thickness. Cut out 12 circles using a round cutter and press each circle into the cups of a tart tin. Spoon the filling into each pastry shell, filling them about two-thirds full.
5. **Air Fry the Tarts:** Place the tart tin in the air fryer basket. Cook for 12-15 minutes, or until the filling is set and the pastry is golden brown. You may need to cook in batches depending on the size of your air fryer.
6. **Serve:** Allow the tarts to cool in the tin for a few minutes before transferring to a wire rack to cool completely. Serve at room temperature.

Tip: For an extra flaky pastry, handle the dough as little as possible and ensure the butter remains cold. Butter tarts can be stored in an airtight container at room temperature for up to three days.

ESTIMATED NUTRITIONAL TABLE PER 100G:

Calories: approx 320 kcal | Fat: approx 18 g | Carbohydrates: approx 40 g | Fibre: approx 1 g | Protein: approx 3 g | Salt: approx 0.3 g

NANAIMO BARS

Nanaimo Bars are a beloved Canadian no-bake dessert named after the city of Nanaimo in British Columbia. They feature three delicious layers: a coconut-graham cracker base, a creamy custard filling, and a rich chocolate topping.

Serves: 12 | Difficulty: Moderate | Prep Time: 30 minutes (plus chilling time) | Cook Time: 5 minutes | Total Time: 35 minutes (plus chilling time)

INGREDIENT LIST:

For the Base:
- 120g unsalted butter, melted
- 50g granulated sugar
- 30g cocoa powder
- 1 large egg, beaten
- 200g digestive biscuits, crushed
- 100g desiccated coconut
- 50g chopped walnuts (optional)

For the Filling:
- 100g unsalted butter, softened
- 250g icing sugar
- 2 tbsp custard powder
- 3 tbsp milk

For the Topping:
- 150g dark chocolate, chopped
- 30g unsalted butter

PREPARATION:

1. **Prepare the Base:** In a medium bowl, combine the melted butter, granulated sugar, and cocoa powder. Stir in the beaten egg until well combined. Add the crushed digestive biscuits, desiccated coconut, and chopped walnuts (if using), and mix until the ingredients are evenly distributed. Press the mixture firmly into the bottom of a lined 20cm square baking tin.
2. **Chill the Base:** Place the tin in the refrigerator for at least 30 minutes to set.
3. **Prepare the Filling:** In a large bowl, beat together the softened butter, icing sugar, custard powder, and milk until smooth and creamy. Spread the filling evenly over the chilled base. Return to the refrigerator to set for another 30 minutes.
4. **Prepare the Topping:** In a heatproof bowl, combine the chopped dark chocolate and butter. Place the bowl in the air fryer at 100 °C (212 °F) for 5 minutes, or until melted. Stir until smooth.
5. **Assemble the Bars:** Pour the melted chocolate mixture over the custard layer, spreading it evenly. Refrigerate for at least 1 hour, or until the chocolate is set.
6. **Serve:** Once fully set, cut into squares or bars. Serve chilled.

Tip: For clean cuts, use a sharp knife warmed under hot water, wiping the blade between each cut. Nanaimo Bars can be stored in an airtight container in the refrigerator for up to one week.

ESTIMATED NUTRITIONAL TABLE PER 100G:
Calories: approx 430 kcal | Fat: approx 28 g | Carbohydrates: approx 42 g | Fibre: approx 3 g | Protein: approx 4 g | Salt: approx 0.3 g

MEXICO

TAQUITOS

Taquitos are a popular Mexican dish consisting of small rolled tortillas filled with a savoury mixture, then fried to crispy perfection. This air fryer version provides a healthier alternative with the same delightful crunch and flavour.

Serves: 4 | Difficulty: Easy | Prep Time: 15 minutes | Cook Time: 10 minutes | Total Time: 25 minutes

INGREDIENT LIST:

- 12 small corn tortillas
- 300g cooked chicken, shredded
- 100g grated cheddar cheese
- 1 small onion, finely chopped
- 1 clove garlic, minced
- 1 tsp ground cumin
- 1 tsp smoked paprika
- 1/2 tsp salt
- 1/2 tsp black pepper
- Cooking spray
- Salsa, guacamole, and sour cream, to serve

PREPARATION:

1. **Prepare the Filling:** In a large bowl, combine the shredded chicken, grated cheddar cheese, chopped onion, minced garlic, ground cumin, smoked paprika, salt, and black pepper. Mix well until all ingredients are evenly distributed.
2. **Warm the Tortillas:** Preheat the air fryer to 180 °C (360 °F). Wrap the corn tortillas in a damp kitchen towel and microwave for 30 seconds to make them pliable.
3. **Assemble the Taquitos:** Place about 2 tablespoons of the chicken mixture along the centre of each tortilla. Roll the tortillas tightly and secure with a toothpick if needed.
4. **Air Fry the Taquitos:** Lightly spray the rolled taquitos with cooking spray. Place them in the air fryer basket in a single layer, seam side down. Cook for 8-10 minutes, turning halfway through, until they are golden and crispy.
5. **Serve:** Remove the toothpicks if used. Serve the taquitos hot with salsa, guacamole, and sour cream on the side.

Tip: For added flavour, you can brush the taquitos with a little lime juice before air frying. To prevent the tortillas from cracking, ensure they are warm and pliable before rolling.

ESTIMATED NUTRITIONAL TABLE PER 100G:
Calories: approx 220 kcal | Fat: approx 10 g | Carbohydrates: approx 20 g | Fibre: approx 2 g | Protein: approx 13 g | Salt: approx 0.8 g

CARNE ASADA TACOS

Carne Asada Tacos are a beloved Mexican street food, featuring marinated and grilled beef served in warm tortillas. This air fryer version ensures the meat is tender and flavourful, perfect for a quick and delicious meal.

Serves: 4 | Difficulty: Moderate | Prep Time: 20 minutes (plus marinating time) | Cook Time: 10 minutes | Total Time: 30 minutes (plus marinating time)

INGREDIENT LIST:

- 500g skirt steak or flank steak
- 2 tbsp olive oil
- 2 tbsp lime juice
- 2 cloves garlic, minced
- 1 tsp ground cumin
- 1 tsp smoked paprika
- 1/2 tsp chilli powder
- 1/2 tsp salt
- 1/2 tsp black pepper
- 8 small corn tortillas
- Fresh coriander, chopped, for garnish
- Diced onions, for garnish
- Lime wedges, for serving
- Salsa, for serving

PREPARATION:

1. **Marinate the Steak:** In a large bowl, combine the olive oil, lime juice, minced garlic, ground cumin, smoked paprika, chilli powder, salt, and black pepper. Add the steak, ensuring it is well coated with the marinade. Cover and refrigerate for at least 1 hour or overnight for best results.
2. **Preheat the Air Fryer:** Preheat the air fryer to 200 °C (390 °F).
3. **Cook the Steak:** Remove the steak from the marinade and pat dry with kitchen paper. Place the steak in the air fryer basket and cook for 8-10 minutes, turning halfway through, until it reaches your desired level of doneness. Let the steak rest for a few minutes before slicing.
4. **Warm the Tortillas:** Wrap the corn tortillas in a damp kitchen towel and microwave for 30 seconds to make them pliable.
5. **Assemble the Tacos:** Slice the steak thinly against the grain. Divide the steak slices among the warm tortillas. Top with fresh coriander, diced onions, and your favourite salsa.
6. **Serve:** Serve the tacos immediately with lime wedges on the side.

Tip: For added flavour, grill the tortillas in the air fryer for a few seconds to give them a slightly crispy texture. You can also add sliced avocado or a dollop of sour cream to the tacos for extra richness.

ESTIMATED NUTRITIONAL TABLE PER 100G:
Calories: approx 200 kcal | Fat: approx 10 g | Carbohydrates: approx 15 g | Fibre: approx 2 g | Protein: approx 12 g | Salt: approx 0.6 g

MEXICAN STREET CORN

Mexican Street Corn, or Elote, is a popular street food in Mexico. It's a flavourful and tangy treat made with grilled corn on the cob, coated in a creamy, cheesy, and spicy mixture. This air fryer version ensures the corn is perfectly cooked and charred.

Serves: 4 | Difficulty: Easy | Prep Time: 10 minutes | Cook Time: 15 minutes | Total Time: 25 minutes

INGREDIENT LIST:

- 4 ears of corn, husked
- 2 tbsp vegetable oil
- 60g mayonnaise
- 60g sour cream
- 50g cotija cheese, crumbled (or feta as a substitute)
- 1 tsp smoked paprika
- 1/2 tsp chilli powder
- 1 lime, cut into wedges
- Fresh coriander, chopped, for garnish
- Salt, to taste

PREPARATION:

1. **Prepare the Corn:** Brush the ears of corn with vegetable oil and season with a pinch of salt.
2. **Preheat the Air Fryer:** Preheat the air fryer to 200 °C (390 °F).
3. **Cook the Corn:** Place the corn in the air fryer basket. Cook for 12-15 minutes, turning halfway through, until the corn is tender and slightly charred.
4. **Prepare the Topping:** In a small bowl, mix together the mayonnaise, sour cream, smoked paprika, and chilli powder.
5. **Assemble the Elote:** Once the corn is cooked, brush each ear with the mayonnaise mixture. Sprinkle with crumbled cotija cheese and chopped coriander.
6. **Serve:** Serve the Mexican Street Corn immediately with lime wedges on the side for squeezing over the top.

Tip: For a bit of extra heat, sprinkle the corn with additional chilli powder or a few dashes of hot sauce. This dish pairs wonderfully with grilled meats and other Mexican dishes.

ESTIMATED NUTRITIONAL TABLE PER 100G:
Calories: approx 150 kcal | Fat: approx 10 g | Carbohydrates: approx 14 g | Fibre: approx 2 g | Protein: approx 3 g | Salt: approx 0.5 g

CHURROS

Churros are a beloved Mexican treat, featuring crispy, golden pastry coated in cinnamon sugar. This air fryer version provides the same delicious crunch and sweetness without the need for deep-frying.

Serves: 4 | Difficulty: Moderate | Prep Time: 15 minutes | Cook Time: 12 minutes | Total Time: 27 minutes

INGREDIENT LIST:

- 120ml water
- 55g unsalted butter
- 1 tbsp granulated sugar
- 1/4 tsp salt
- 70g plain flour
- 1 large egg
- 1/2 tsp vanilla extract
- Cooking spray
- 100g granulated sugar
- 1 tsp ground cinnamon

PREPARATION:

1. **Prepare the Dough:** In a medium saucepan, combine the water, butter, 1 tbsp granulated sugar, and salt. Bring to a boil over medium heat. Add the flour all at once and stir vigorously until the mixture forms a ball and pulls away from the sides of the pan. Remove from heat and let cool for 5 minutes.
2. **Add the Egg:** Once the dough has cooled slightly, add the egg and vanilla extract. Stir until the mixture is smooth and glossy. Transfer the dough to a piping bag fitted with a star tip.
3. **Preheat the Air Fryer:** Preheat the air fryer to 180 °C (360 °F).
4. **Pipe and Cook the Churros:** Pipe 10cm strips of dough onto a parchment-lined baking tray. Lightly spray the churros with cooking spray. Place them in the air fryer basket in a single layer. Cook for 10-12 minutes, or until golden and crisp, turning halfway through.
5. **Coat in Cinnamon Sugar:** In a shallow dish, mix the remaining 100g of granulated sugar with the ground cinnamon. While the churros are still warm, roll them in the cinnamon sugar until well coated.
6. **Serve:** Serve the churros immediately with a side of chocolate sauce for dipping if desired.

Tip: For a richer flavour, you can add a pinch of ground nutmeg to the dough. Make sure to pipe the churros evenly to ensure they cook uniformly.

ESTIMATED NUTRITIONAL TABLE PER 100G:

Calories: approx 260 kcal | Fat: approx 10 g | Carbohydrates: approx 38 g | Fibre: approx 1 g | Protein: approx 3 g | Salt: approx 0.3 g

CHAPTER 2: SOUTH AMERICA

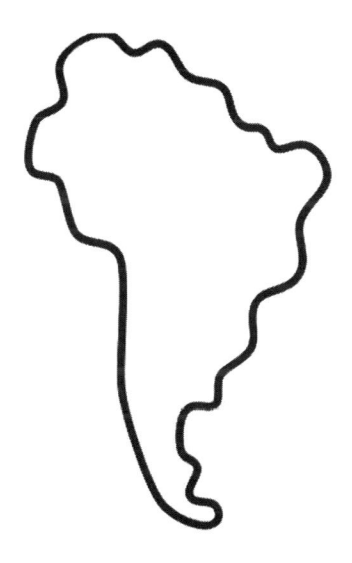

BRAZIL

COXINHA (CHICKEN CROQUETTES)

Coxinha is a popular Brazilian street food, featuring a crispy outer shell filled with a savoury chicken mixture. These chicken croquettes are traditionally deep-fried, but this air fryer version provides the same delicious flavour with less oil.

Serves: 4 | Difficulty: Moderate | Prep Time: 30 minutes | Cook Time: 20 minutes | Total Time: 50 minutes

INGREDIENT LIST:

For the Filling:
- 300g cooked chicken breast, shredded
- 1 small onion, finely chopped
- 2 cloves garlic, minced
- 2 tbsp olive oil
- 1/2 tsp smoked paprika
- 1/2 tsp ground cumin
- Salt and pepper, to taste
- 2 tbsp cream cheese
- Fresh parsley, chopped (optional)

For the Dough:
- 250ml chicken stock
- 250ml whole milk
- 2 tbsp butter
- 250g plain flour
- Salt, to taste

For the Coating:
- 2 large eggs, beaten
- 100g breadcrumbs
- Cooking spray

PREPARATION:

1. **Prepare the Filling:** In a large pan, heat the olive oil over medium heat. Add the chopped onion and garlic, and cook until softened. Add the shredded chicken, smoked paprika, ground cumin, salt, and pepper. Stir well to combine. Remove from heat and mix in the cream cheese and chopped parsley. Set aside to cool.
2. **Prepare the Dough:** In a large saucepan, combine the chicken stock, milk, butter, and a pinch of salt. Bring to a boil. Add the flour all at once, stirring vigorously until the dough comes together and pulls away from the sides of the pan. Remove from heat and let it cool slightly.
3. **Form the Coxinhas:** Take a small amount of dough and flatten it in your hand. Place a spoonful of the chicken filling in the centre and shape the dough around the filling to form a teardrop shape. Repeat with the remaining dough and filling.
4. **Coat the Coxinhas:** Dip each coxinha into the beaten eggs, then roll in breadcrumbs to coat evenly.
5. **Preheat the Air Fryer:** Preheat the air fryer to 180 °C (360 °F).
6. **Air Fry the Coxinhas:** Lightly spray the coxinhas with cooking spray. Place them in the air fryer basket in a single layer. Cook for 15-20 minutes, turning halfway through, until golden and crispy.
7. **Serve:** Serve the coxinhas hot, accompanied by a dipping sauce of your choice.

Tip: For extra flavour, you can add a pinch of cayenne pepper to the chicken filling. Make sure to seal the dough well around the filling to prevent any leakage during cooking.

ESTIMATED NUTRITIONAL TABLE PER 100G:
Calories: approx 220 kcal | Fat: approx 10 g | Carbohydrates: approx 20 g | Fibre: approx 1 g | Protein: approx 12 g | Salt: approx 0.7 g

FEIJOADA (BLACK BEAN STEW)

Feijoada is a traditional Brazilian black bean stew, typically made with a variety of meats and slow-cooked to perfection. This air fryer version simplifies the process while preserving the rich, hearty flavours of this beloved dish.

Serves: 4 | Difficulty: Moderate | Prep Time: 20 minutes | Cook Time: 35 minutes | Total Time: 55 minutes

INGREDIENT LIST:

- 200g dried black beans, soaked overnight and drained
- 200g pork shoulder, cut into cubes
- 150g chorizo sausage, sliced
- 1 onion, finely chopped
- 2 cloves garlic, minced
- 1 bay leaf
- 1 tsp smoked paprika
- 1 tsp ground cumin
- 1/2 tsp chilli flakes
- 400ml chicken stock
- 1 tbsp olive oil
- Salt and pepper, to taste
- Fresh coriander, chopped, for garnish
- Orange slices, for serving
- Cooked white rice, for serving

PREPARATION:

1. **Preheat the Air Fryer:** Preheat the air fryer to 180 °C (360 °F).
2. **Cook the Meats:** In a large, air fryer-safe dish, combine the pork shoulder and chorizo. Drizzle with olive oil and cook in the air fryer for 15 minutes, stirring halfway through, until browned.
3. **Add Aromatics:** Add the chopped onion and minced garlic to the dish with the meats. Cook for an additional 5 minutes until the onion is softened.
4. **Add Beans and Seasonings:** Stir in the soaked and drained black beans, bay leaf, smoked paprika, ground cumin, and chilli flakes. Pour in the chicken stock and stir to combine.
5. **Cook the Stew:** Cover the dish with foil and cook in the air fryer at 180 °C (360 °F) for 15-20 minutes, until the beans are tender and the stew is thickened. Check halfway through and add more stock if necessary to keep the beans submerged.
6. **Season and Serve:** Remove the bay leaf and season the stew with salt and pepper to taste. Garnish with fresh coriander and serve with orange slices and cooked white rice.

Tip: For an even richer flavour, let the stew rest for a few hours or overnight in the refrigerator before reheating and serving. This allows the flavours to meld together beautifully.

ESTIMATED NUTRITIONAL TABLE PER 100G:

Calories: approx 180 kcal | Fat: approx 10 g | Carbohydrates: approx 15 g | Fibre: approx 4 g | Protein: approx 9 g | Salt: approx 0.8 g

PÃO DE QUEIJO (CHEESE BREAD)

Pão de Queijo, or Brazilian cheese bread, is a popular snack made from tapioca flour and cheese. These small, chewy rolls are naturally gluten-free and have a deliciously cheesy flavour. This air fryer version makes them quick and easy to prepare.

Serves: 4 | Difficulty: Easy | Prep Time: 15 minutes | Cook Time: 15 minutes | Total Time: 30 minutes

INGREDIENT LIST:

- 250g tapioca flour
- 120ml milk
- 60ml water
- 60ml vegetable oil
- 1/2 tsp salt
- 100g grated parmesan cheese
- 100g grated mozzarella cheese
- 2 large eggs

PREPARATION:

1. **Preheat the Air Fryer:** Preheat the air fryer to 180 °C (360 °F).
2. **Heat the Liquids:** In a saucepan, combine the milk, water, vegetable oil, and salt. Bring to a boil over medium heat.
3. **Mix the Dough:** Place the tapioca flour in a large bowl. Pour the hot milk mixture over the flour and stir until well combined. Allow the mixture to cool for a few minutes.
4. **Add the Cheese and Eggs:** Once the dough is cool enough to handle, add the grated parmesan and mozzarella cheeses. Mix in the eggs until the dough is smooth and well combined. The dough will be sticky.
5. **Shape the Dough:** Lightly oil your hands and form the dough into small balls, about the size of a golf ball.
6. **Air Fry the Pão de Queijo:** Place the dough balls in the air fryer basket, leaving space between each one to allow for expansion. Cook for 12-15 minutes, until the cheese bread is golden and puffed.
7. **Serve:** Serve the Pão de Queijo warm, either on their own or with a dipping sauce.

Tip: For an extra burst of flavour, you can add a pinch of garlic powder or dried herbs to the dough. These cheese breads are best enjoyed fresh from the air fryer but can be reheated in the air fryer for a few minutes if needed.

ESTIMATED NUTRITIONAL TABLE PER 100G:
Calories: approx 300 kcal | Fat: approx 15 g | Carbohydrates: approx 30 g | Fibre: approx 1 g | Protein: approx 10 g | Salt: approx 0.8 g

BRIGADEIROS

Brigadeiros are a traditional Brazilian sweet treat, similar to truffles, made from condensed milk, cocoa powder, and butter. They are typically rolled in chocolate sprinkles and are a staple at Brazilian celebrations. This air fryer version ensures a quick and easy preparation.

Serves: 4 | Difficulty: Easy | Prep Time: 10 minutes | Cook Time: 10 minutes (plus cooling time) | Total Time: 20 minutes

INGREDIENT LIST:

- 1 can (397g) sweetened condensed milk
- 2 tbsp unsweetened cocoa powder
- 2 tbsp unsalted butter
- Pinch of salt
- Chocolate sprinkles, for rolling

PREPARATION:

1. **Mix the Ingredients:** In a large, air fryer-safe bowl, combine the sweetened condensed milk, cocoa powder, unsalted butter, and a pinch of salt. Mix well until smooth.
2. **Cook the Mixture:** Preheat the air fryer to 160 °C (320 °F). Place the bowl with the mixture in the air fryer basket and cook for 10 minutes, stirring every 2-3 minutes, until the mixture thickens and starts to pull away from the sides of the bowl.
3. **Cool the Mixture:** Remove the bowl from the air fryer and let the mixture cool to room temperature. Once cool, refrigerate for at least 30 minutes to firm up.
4. **Form the Brigadeiros:** Grease your hands with a bit of butter to prevent sticking. Scoop out small amounts of the mixture and roll into balls about the size of a walnut.
5. **Roll in Sprinkles:** Roll each ball in chocolate sprinkles until fully coated.
6. **Serve:** Arrange the Brigadeiros on a serving plate and serve at room temperature.

Tip: For a variation, you can roll the Brigadeiros in desiccated coconut, crushed nuts, or cocoa powder. Store any leftovers in an airtight container in the refrigerator for up to one week.

ESTIMATED NUTRITIONAL TABLE PER 100G:
Calories: approx 350 kcal | Fat: approx 12 g | Carbohydrates: approx 55 g | Fibre: approx 1 g | Protein: approx 6 g | Salt: approx 0.2 g

ARGENTINA

EMPANADAS

Empanadas are a popular Argentine pastry filled with a savoury mixture of meat, onions, and spices. They are traditionally baked or fried, but this air fryer version offers a healthier and equally delicious alternative with a crispy crust and flavourful filling.

Serves: 4 | Difficulty: Moderate | Prep Time: 30 minutes | Cook Time: 15 minutes | Total Time: 45 minutes

INGREDIENT LIST:

For the Dough:
- 300g plain flour
- 1 tsp salt
- 100g cold unsalted butter, cubed
- 1 egg
- 60ml cold water

For the Filling:
- 250g minced beef
- 1 onion, finely chopped
- 2 cloves garlic, minced
- 1 red bell pepper, finely chopped
- 1 hard-boiled egg, chopped
- 50g green olives, chopped
- 1 tsp smoked paprika
- 1 tsp ground cumin
- 1/2 tsp chilli flakes (optional)
- Salt and pepper, to taste
- 2 tbsp vegetable oil

For Assembly:
- 1 egg, beaten (for egg wash)

PREPARATION:
1. **Make the Dough:** In a large bowl, mix the flour and salt. Add the cold butter and rub it into the flour until the mixture resembles coarse crumbs. Beat the egg with the cold water and add to the flour mixture. Mix until the dough comes together. Wrap the dough in cling film and refrigerate for at least 30 minutes.
2. **Prepare the Filling:** In a large pan, heat the vegetable oil over medium heat. Add the chopped onion, garlic, and red bell pepper. Cook until softened. Add the minced beef, smoked paprika, ground cumin, and chilli flakes if using. Cook until the beef is browned. Stir in the chopped hard-boiled egg and green olives. Season with salt and pepper to taste. Allow the filling to cool.
3. **Preheat the Air Fryer:** Preheat the air fryer to 180 °C (360 °F).
4. **Assemble the Empanadas:** Roll out the dough on a floured surface to about 3mm thickness. Cut out circles of dough using a round cutter (about 10-12cm in diameter). Place a spoonful of the filling in the centre of each circle. Fold the dough over to enclose the filling and crimp the edges with a fork to seal. Brush the empanadas with the beaten egg.
5. **Air Fry the Empanadas:** Place the empanadas in the air fryer basket in a single layer. Cook for 12-15 minutes, or until the crust is golden and crispy.
6. **Serve:** Allow the empanadas to cool slightly before serving. Enjoy them warm.

Tip: For added flavour, you can mix a little bit of cheese into the filling. These empanadas can be served with a side of chimichurri sauce for dipping.

ESTIMATED NUTRITIONAL TABLE PER 100G:
Calories: approx 260 kcal | Fat: approx 15 g | Carbohydrates: approx 20 g | Fibre: approx 1 g | Protein: approx 10 g | Salt: approx 0.8 g

ASADO (GRILLED BEEF)

Asado is a traditional Argentine dish, typically featuring beef grilled to perfection. This air fryer version captures the essence of asado, offering tender and juicy beef with a deliciously charred exterior.

Serves: 4 | Difficulty: Moderate | Prep Time: 15 minutes (plus marinating time) | Cook Time: 20 minutes | Total Time: 35 minutes (plus marinating time)

INGREDIENT LIST:

- 600g beef ribs or flank steak
- 2 tbsp olive oil
- 3 cloves garlic, minced
- 1 tbsp fresh rosemary, chopped
- 1 tbsp fresh thyme, chopped
- 1 tsp smoked paprika
- 1 tsp salt
- 1/2 tsp black pepper
- Juice of 1 lemon

PREPARATION:

1. **Marinate the Beef:** In a large bowl, mix the olive oil, minced garlic, fresh rosemary, fresh thyme, smoked paprika, salt, black pepper, and lemon juice. Add the beef, ensuring it is well coated with the marinade. Cover and refrigerate for at least 1 hour, preferably overnight.
2. **Preheat the Air Fryer:** Preheat the air fryer to 200 °C (390 °F).
3. **Cook the Beef:** Remove the beef from the marinade and pat dry with kitchen paper. Place the beef in the air fryer basket. Cook for 18-20 minutes, turning halfway through, until the beef reaches your desired level of doneness. The internal temperature should reach at least 63 °C (145 °F) for medium-rare.
4. **Rest the Beef:** Transfer the beef to a cutting board and let it rest for 5 minutes before slicing.
5. **Serve:** Slice the beef against the grain and serve immediately.

Tip: For an authentic touch, serve the asado with chimichurri sauce and a side of grilled vegetables. Ensure the beef is not overcrowded in the air fryer basket to allow for even cooking.

ESTIMATED NUTRITIONAL TABLE PER 100G:

Calories: approx 250 kcal | Fat: approx 15 g | Carbohydrates: approx 2 g | Fibre: approx 0 g | Protein: approx 25 g | Salt: approx 0.7 g

CHIMICHURRI POTATOES

Chimichurri Potatoes combine the vibrant flavours of Argentina's famous chimichurri sauce with crispy roasted potatoes. This air fryer recipe makes a perfect side dish, offering a delightful blend of herbs and spices.

Serves: 4 | Difficulty: Easy | Prep Time: 10 minutes | Cook Time: 20 minutes | Total Time: 30 minutes

INGREDIENT LIST:

- 600g baby potatoes, halved
- 2 tbsp olive oil
- 1 tsp salt
- 1/2 tsp black pepper

For the Chimichurri Sauce:
- 1 bunch fresh parsley, finely chopped
- 4 cloves garlic, minced
- 2 tbsp fresh oregano, finely chopped
- 1 red chilli, finely chopped
- 60ml red wine vinegar
- 120ml olive oil
- 1 tsp salt
- 1/2 tsp black pepper

PREPARATION:

1. **Preheat the Air Fryer:** Preheat the air fryer to 200 °C (390 °F).
2. **Prepare the Potatoes:** In a large bowl, toss the halved baby potatoes with olive oil, salt, and black pepper. Ensure they are evenly coated.
3. **Air Fry the Potatoes:** Place the potatoes in the air fryer basket in a single layer. Cook for 18-20 minutes, shaking the basket halfway through, until the potatoes are golden and crispy.
4. **Make the Chimichurri Sauce:** While the potatoes are cooking, prepare the chimichurri sauce. In a bowl, combine the finely chopped parsley, minced garlic, chopped oregano, chopped red chilli, red wine vinegar, olive oil, salt, and black pepper. Mix well.
5. **Toss with Chimichurri:** Once the potatoes are cooked, transfer them to a serving bowl. Drizzle with the chimichurri sauce and toss to coat evenly.
6. **Serve:** Serve the chimichurri potatoes immediately as a side dish.

Tip: For a milder chimichurri, remove the seeds from the chilli before chopping. The sauce can be made in advance and stored in the refrigerator for up to one week.

ESTIMATED NUTRITIONAL TABLE PER 100G:
Calories: approx 150 kcal | Fat: approx 10 g | Carbohydrates: approx 15 g | Fibre: approx 2 g | Protein: approx 2 g | Salt: approx 0.5 g

ALFAJORES

Alfajores are traditional Argentine biscuits filled with dulce de leche and rolled in coconut. These tender, crumbly treats are beloved throughout South America and make a delightful dessert or snack.

Serves: 4 | Difficulty: Moderate | Prep Time: 20 minutes | Cook Time: 10 minutes (plus cooling time) | Total Time: 30 minutes (plus cooling time)

INGREDIENT LIST:

For the Biscuits:
- 150g plain flour
- 100g cornflour (cornstarch)
- 1 tsp baking powder
- 100g unsalted butter, softened
- 75g caster sugar
- 2 large egg yolks
- 1 tsp vanilla extract
- 1 tbsp milk (if needed)

For the Filling:
- 200g dulce de leche

For Assembly:
- 50g desiccated coconut

PREPARATION:

1. **Make the Biscuit Dough:** In a bowl, sift together the plain flour, cornflour, and baking powder. In another bowl, cream the softened butter and caster sugar until light and fluffy. Add the egg yolks and vanilla extract, and mix well. Gradually add the flour mixture to the butter mixture, mixing until a soft dough forms. If the dough is too dry, add a tablespoon of milk.
2. **Preheat the Air Fryer:** Preheat the air fryer to 160 °C (320 °F).
3. **Shape the Biscuits:** Roll out the dough on a floured surface to about 5mm thickness. Use a round cutter (about 5cm in diameter) to cut out biscuits. Place the biscuits on a parchment-lined tray.
4. **Air Fry the Biscuits:** Place the biscuits in the air fryer basket in a single layer. Cook for 8-10 minutes, or until they are lightly golden. Let them cool completely on a wire rack.
5. **Assemble the Alfajores:** Once the biscuits are cool, spread a generous amount of dulce de leche on the flat side of half of the biscuits. Top with the remaining biscuits to form sandwiches.
6. **Roll in Coconut:** Roll the edges of the alfajores in desiccated coconut to coat the dulce de leche.
7. **Serve:** Serve the alfajores immediately or store in an airtight container for up to a week.

Tip: For an extra indulgent treat, dip half of each alfajor in melted chocolate and allow to set before serving. Ensure the biscuits are completely cool before filling to prevent the dulce de leche from melting.

ESTIMATED NUTRITIONAL TABLE PER 100G:

Calories: approx 360 kcal | Fat: approx 18 g | Carbohydrates: approx 45 g | Fibre: approx 2 g | Protein: approx 4 g | Salt: approx 0.2 g

PERU

CEVICHE TOSTADAS

Ceviche Tostadas are a refreshing and vibrant Peruvian dish, combining marinated fish with crispy tostadas. This air fryer version ensures the tostadas are perfectly crisp while the ceviche offers a zesty and fresh contrast.

Serves: 4 | Difficulty: Moderate | Prep Time: 20 minutes (plus marinating time) | Cook Time: 8 minutes | Total Time: 28 minutes (plus marinating time)

INGREDIENT LIST:

For the Tostadas:
- 8 small corn tortillas
- Cooking spray
- Salt, to taste

For the Ceviche:
- 300g fresh white fish fillets (such as sea bass or cod), diced
- 120ml fresh lime juice
- 1 red onion, finely sliced
- 1 red chilli, finely chopped
- 1 large tomato, diced
- 1 small cucumber, diced
- 2 tbsp fresh coriander, chopped
- Salt and pepper, to taste

For Garnish:
- Fresh avocado slices
- Extra coriander, chopped
- Lime wedges

PREPARATION:

1. **Prepare the Tostadas:** Preheat the air fryer to 180 °C (360 °F). Lightly spray both sides of the corn tortillas with cooking spray and sprinkle with a pinch of salt. Place the tortillas in the air fryer basket in a single layer. Cook for 6-8 minutes, flipping halfway through, until they are golden and crispy. Remove and let cool.
2. **Prepare the Ceviche:** In a glass or ceramic bowl, combine the diced fish and lime juice. Stir in the red onion and chilli. Cover and refrigerate for at least 15-20 minutes, or until the fish is opaque and „cooked" by the lime juice.
3. **Add Vegetables to Ceviche:** Once the fish is marinated, drain off some of the excess lime juice. Add the diced tomato, cucumber, and chopped coriander to the fish mixture. Season with salt and pepper to taste.
4. **Assemble the Tostadas:** Spoon the ceviche mixture onto the crispy tostadas. Top with fresh avocado slices and a sprinkle of extra coriander.
5. **Serve:** Serve the ceviche tostadas immediately with lime wedges on the side for squeezing over the top.

Tip: For added flavour, you can mix a splash of orange juice into the lime juice for marinating the fish. Make sure to serve the tostadas immediately after assembling to maintain their crispiness.

ESTIMATED NUTRITIONAL TABLE PER 100G:
Calories: approx 150 kcal | Fat: approx 5 g | Carbohydrates: approx 15 g | Fibre: approx 2 g | Protein: approx 10 g | Salt: approx 0.5 g

LOMO SALTADO

Lomo Saltado is a popular Peruvian dish that combines marinated beef, vegetables, and crispy chips, showcasing a fusion of Peruvian and Asian flavours. This air fryer version offers a quick and healthy way to enjoy this delicious stir-fry.

Serves: 4 | Difficulty: Moderate | Prep Time: 20 minutes | Cook Time: 25 minutes | Total Time: 45 minutes

INGREDIENT LIST:

- 500g beef sirloin, cut into thin strips
- 4 large potatoes, cut into chips
- 2 tbsp olive oil
- 1 red onion, sliced
- 2 tomatoes, cut into wedges
- 1 red bell pepper, sliced
- 2 cloves garlic, minced
- 3 tbsp soy sauce
- 2 tbsp red wine vinegar
- 1 tbsp oyster sauce
- 1 tsp ground cumin
- Salt and pepper, to taste
- Fresh coriander, chopped, for garnish
- Cooked white rice, for serving

PREPARATION:

1. **Preheat the Air Fryer:** Preheat the air fryer to 200 °C (390 °F).
2. **Prepare the Chips:** Toss the cut potatoes with 1 tbsp of olive oil and a pinch of salt. Place them in the air fryer basket in a single layer. Cook for 20-25 minutes, shaking the basket halfway through, until golden and crispy. Remove and keep warm.
3. **Marinate the Beef:** In a bowl, combine the beef strips with soy sauce, red wine vinegar, oyster sauce, ground cumin, and minced garlic. Let it marinate for at least 15 minutes.
4. **Cook the Beef and Vegetables:** In an air fryer-safe pan or dish, heat the remaining 1 tbsp of olive oil. Add the marinated beef strips and cook at 200 °C (390 °F) for 5-7 minutes until browned. Add the sliced red onion, red bell pepper, and tomato wedges. Cook for an additional 5 minutes, until the vegetables are tender but still crisp.
5. **Combine and Serve:** Toss the cooked chips with the beef and vegetable mixture. Garnish with chopped fresh coriander. Serve the Lomo Saltado immediately with cooked white rice.

Tip: For an extra flavour boost, add a splash of lime juice just before serving. Ensure the air fryer is preheated for optimal cooking and crispiness.

ESTIMATED NUTRITIONAL TABLE PER 100G:

Calories: approx 180 kcal | Fat: approx 8 g | Carbohydrates: approx 15 g | Fibre: approx 2 g | Protein: approx 12 g | Salt: approx 1.0 g

PERUVIAN CORN

Peruvian Corn, known as Choclo, is a staple in Peruvian cuisine. This dish highlights the large, tender kernels of Peruvian corn, seasoned and roasted to perfection. The air fryer version brings out the natural sweetness and adds a delightful char.

Serves: 4 | Difficulty: Easy | Prep Time: 10 minutes | Cook Time: 15 minutes | Total Time: 25 minutes

INGREDIENT LIST:

- 4 ears of Peruvian corn (Choclo), husked and cut into rounds
- 2 tbsp olive oil
- 1 tsp salt
- 1/2 tsp black pepper
- 1 tsp paprika
- 1 tsp dried oregano
- Fresh lime wedges, for serving

PREPARATION:

1. **Preheat the Air Fryer:** Preheat the air fryer to 200 °C (390 °F).
2. **Season the Corn:** In a large bowl, toss the corn rounds with olive oil, salt, black pepper, paprika, and dried oregano until evenly coated.
3. **Air Fry the Corn:** Place the seasoned corn rounds in the air fryer basket in a single layer. Cook for 12-15 minutes, shaking the basket halfway through, until the corn is tender and slightly charred.
4. **Serve:** Transfer the roasted corn to a serving platter and serve immediately with fresh lime wedges on the side.

Tip: For an extra burst of flavour, sprinkle the corn with grated cheese or a drizzle of your favourite hot sauce before serving. If Peruvian corn is unavailable, you can substitute with standard sweetcorn, though the texture and size will differ.

ESTIMATED NUTRITIONAL TABLE PER 100G:

Calories: approx 120 kcal | Fat: approx 5 g | Carbohydrates: approx 18 g | Fibre: approx 2 g | Protein: approx 3 g | Salt: approx 0.7 g

PICARONES (PUMPKIN DONUTS)

Picarones are a traditional Peruvian dessert made from a dough of pumpkin and sweet potato, fried to a golden crisp and drizzled with a sweet syrup. This air fryer version offers a healthier take on these delicious pumpkin donuts.

Serves: 4 | Difficulty: Moderate | Prep Time: 20 minutes (plus resting time) | Cook Time: 15 minutes | Total Time: 35 minutes (plus resting time)

INGREDIENT LIST:

For the Dough:
- 200g pumpkin, peeled and cubed
- 200g sweet potato, peeled and cubed
- 250g plain flour
- 1 tsp instant yeast
- 2 tbsp caster sugar
- 1/2 tsp salt
- 1/2 tsp ground cinnamon
- 1/4 tsp ground anise
- 1 large egg
- 1 tbsp vegetable oil

For the Syrup:
- 200g dark brown sugar
- 120ml water
- 1 cinnamon stick
- 2 cloves
- 1 star anise

PREPARATION:

1. **Cook the Vegetables:** In a saucepan, cook the pumpkin and sweet potato in boiling water until tender, about 15 minutes. Drain and mash until smooth. Let cool slightly.
2. **Make the Dough:** In a large bowl, combine the mashed pumpkin and sweet potato with the flour, instant yeast, caster sugar, salt, ground cinnamon, and ground anise. Add the egg and vegetable oil, mixing until a sticky dough forms. Cover and let the dough rest in a warm place for 1 hour, or until doubled in size.
3. **Preheat the Air Fryer:** Preheat the air fryer to 180 °C (360 °F).
4. **Shape the Picarones:** Lightly oil your hands and form the dough into small rings or donut shapes.
5. **Air Fry the Picarones:** Place the picarones in the air fryer basket in a single layer, ensuring they do not touch. Cook for 12-15 minutes, turning halfway through, until golden and cooked through.
6. **Prepare the Syrup:** While the picarones are cooking, combine the dark brown sugar, water, cinnamon stick, cloves, and star anise in a saucepan. Bring to a boil, then reduce the heat and simmer for 10 minutes until thickened. Remove the spices before serving.
7. **Serve:** Drizzle the picarones with the warm syrup and serve immediately.

Tip: For an extra touch of sweetness, you can dust the picarones with icing sugar before drizzling with syrup. Ensure the dough has properly rested and risen to achieve a light and fluffy texture.

ESTIMATED NUTRITIONAL TABLE PER 100G:
Calories: approx 250 kcal | Fat: approx 5 g | Carbohydrates: approx 50 g | Fibre: approx 3 g | Protein: approx 4 g | Salt: approx 0.3 g

CHAPTER 3: EUROPE

ITALY

BRUSCHETTA

Bruschetta is a classic Italian appetiser featuring toasted bread topped with a fresh tomato and basil mixture. This air fryer version ensures perfectly crisp bread with a vibrant, flavourful topping.

Serves: 4 | Difficulty: Easy | Prep Time: 10 minutes | Cook Time: 8 minutes | Total Time: 18 minutes

INGREDIENT LIST:

- 1 baguette, sliced into 1.5 cm thick slices
- 2 tbsp olive oil
- 4 ripe tomatoes, diced
- 2 cloves garlic, minced
- 1 tbsp balsamic vinegar
- 1 handful fresh basil leaves, chopped
- Salt and pepper, to taste
- 1 clove garlic, halved (for rubbing on bread)
- Extra basil leaves, for garnish

PREPARATION:

1. **Prepare the Bread:** Brush both sides of the baguette slices with olive oil. Place them in the air fryer basket in a single layer.
2. **Air Fry the Bread:** Preheat the air fryer to 180 °C (360 °F). Cook the bread slices for 5-8 minutes, or until golden and crispy. Remove and let cool slightly.
3. **Prepare the Topping:** In a medium bowl, combine the diced tomatoes, minced garlic, balsamic vinegar, chopped basil, salt, and pepper. Mix well.
4. **Rub with Garlic:** Once the bread slices are cool enough to handle, rub the cut side of the halved garlic clove over one side of each slice.
5. **Assemble the Bruschetta:** Spoon the tomato mixture onto the garlic-rubbed side of each toasted bread slice.
6. **Serve:** Garnish with extra basil leaves and serve immediately.

Tip: For added flavour, you can drizzle a little extra virgin olive oil over the top of the assembled bruschetta. Ensure the bread is toasted just right for a perfect crunchy texture that holds the topping well.

ESTIMATED NUTRITIONAL TABLE PER 100G:

Calories: approx 200 kcal | Fat: approx 8 g | Carbohydrates: approx 25 g | Fibre: approx 2 g | Protein: approx 4 g | Salt: approx 0.5 g

CHICKEN PARMESAN

Chicken Parmesan, or "Chicken Parmigiana", is a classic Italian-American dish featuring breaded chicken cutlets topped with marinara sauce and melted cheese. This air fryer version ensures a crispy coating and juicy chicken without the need for deep-frying.

Serves: 4 | Difficulty: Moderate | Prep Time: 15 minutes | Cook Time: 20 minutes | Total Time: 35 minutes

INGREDIENT LIST:

- 2 large chicken breasts, halved horizontally to make 4 cutlets
- 100g plain flour
- 2 large eggs, beaten
- 100g breadcrumbs
- 50g grated Parmesan cheese
- 1 tsp dried oregano
- 1 tsp garlic powder
- Salt and pepper, to taste
- 200ml marinara sauce
- 100g mozzarella cheese, sliced
- 2 tbsp olive oil
- Fresh basil leaves, for garnish

PREPARATION:

1. **Prepare the Breading Stations:** Set up three shallow bowls: one with plain flour, one with beaten eggs, and one with a mixture of breadcrumbs, grated Parmesan cheese, dried oregano, garlic powder, salt, and pepper.
2. **Bread the Chicken:** Dredge each chicken cutlet in the flour, shaking off any excess. Dip in the beaten eggs, then coat with the breadcrumb mixture, pressing lightly to adhere.
3. **Preheat the Air Fryer:** Preheat the air fryer to 200 °C (390 °F).
4. **Air Fry the Chicken:** Lightly spray the air fryer basket with cooking spray. Place the breaded chicken cutlets in the basket in a single layer. Lightly spray the tops with cooking spray. Cook for 10 minutes, flipping halfway through, until the chicken is golden and crispy.
5. **Add Sauce and Cheese:** Spoon marinara sauce over each chicken cutlet and top with slices of mozzarella cheese. Return to the air fryer and cook for an additional 5 minutes, or until the cheese is melted and bubbly.
6. **Serve:** Garnish with fresh basil leaves and serve immediately.

Tip: For extra flavour, you can add a sprinkle of crushed red pepper flakes to the marinara sauce. Serve with a side of spaghetti or a fresh green salad for a complete meal.

ESTIMATED NUTRITIONAL TABLE PER 100G:
Calories: approx 240 kcal | Fat: approx 12 g | Carbohydrates: approx 12 g | Fibre: approx 1 g | Protein: approx 20 g | Salt: approx 0.8 g

GARLIC BREAD

Garlic Bread is a beloved Italian side dish featuring crusty bread slathered with a rich garlic butter spread. This air fryer version ensures perfectly toasted bread with a delicious garlic flavour.

Serves: 4 | Difficulty: Easy | Prep Time: 10 minutes | Cook Time: 8 minutes | Total Time: 18 minutes

INGREDIENT LIST:

- 1 baguette or Italian bread, sliced in half lengthwise
- 100g unsalted butter, softened
- 4 cloves garlic, minced
- 2 tbsp fresh parsley, chopped
- 1/2 tsp salt
- 1/4 tsp black pepper
- 50g grated Parmesan cheese (optional)

PREPARATION:

1. **Prepare the Garlic Butter:** In a bowl, mix the softened butter, minced garlic, chopped parsley, salt, and black pepper until well combined.
2. **Spread the Butter:** Spread the garlic butter mixture evenly over the cut sides of the bread. If using, sprinkle the grated Parmesan cheese over the top.
3. **Preheat the Air Fryer:** Preheat the air fryer to 180 °C (360 °F).
4. **Air Fry the Bread:** Place the bread halves in the air fryer basket, cut side up. Cook for 6-8 minutes, or until the bread is golden and crispy, and the garlic butter is melted and bubbly.
5. **Serve:** Slice the garlic bread and serve immediately.

Tip: For a twist, you can add a sprinkle of dried Italian herbs to the garlic butter mixture. Serve the garlic bread alongside pasta dishes, soups, or salads.

ESTIMATED NUTRITIONAL TABLE PER 100G:

Calories: approx 300 kcal | Fat: approx 18 g | Carbohydrates: approx 30 g | Fibre: approx 2 g | Protein: approx 6 g | Salt: approx 0.7 g

TIRAMISU BITES

Tiramisu Bites are a delightful twist on the classic Italian dessert, featuring creamy mascarpone filling sandwiched between layers of coffee-soaked sponge, then coated in cocoa powder. These bite-sized treats are perfect for parties and gatherings.

Serves: 4 | Difficulty: Moderate | Prep Time: 20 minutes (plus chilling time) | Cook Time: 10 minutes | Total Time: 30 minutes (plus chilling time)

INGREDIENT LIST:

For the Sponge Cake:
- 3 large eggs
- 75g caster sugar
- 75g plain flour
- 1 tsp baking powder
- 1/2 tsp vanilla extract

For the Filling:
- 250g mascarpone cheese
- 100ml double cream
- 50g icing sugar
- 1 tsp vanilla extract

For the Coffee Soak:
- 100ml strong brewed coffee, cooled
- 2 tbsp coffee liqueur (optional)

For Assembly:
- Cocoa powder, for dusting

PREPARATION:
1. **Preheat the Air Fryer:** Preheat the air fryer to 160 °C (320 °F). Line a small baking tray with parchment paper.
2. **Make the Sponge Cake:** In a large bowl, whisk the eggs and caster sugar until pale and fluffy. Gently fold in the plain flour, baking powder, and vanilla extract until well combined. Pour the batter into the prepared baking tray and spread evenly.
3. **Air Fry the Sponge:** Place the tray in the air fryer basket and cook for 8-10 minutes, or until the sponge is golden, and a skewer inserted into the centre comes out clean. Let the sponge cool completely.
4. **Prepare the Filling:** In a bowl, beat the mascarpone cheese, double cream, icing sugar, and vanilla extract until smooth and thick.
5. **Cut the Sponge:** Once cooled, cut the sponge cake into small, bite-sized squares.
6. **Assemble the Tiramisu Bites:** Dip each sponge square briefly into the cooled coffee mixture. Sandwich a dollop of the mascarpone filling between two coffee-soaked sponge squares to form a bite-sized piece. Repeat with the remaining squares and filling.
7. **Chill:** Arrange the tiramisu bites on a tray and refrigerate for at least 1 hour to set.
8. **Serve:** Just before serving, dust the tiramisu bites with cocoa powder.

Tip: For an extra touch of elegance, you can pipe the mascarpone filling using a piping bag with a star nozzle. These bites are best served chilled and can be stored in the refrigerator for up to two days.

ESTIMATED NUTRITIONAL TABLE PER 100G:
Calories: approx 300 kcal | Fat: approx 20 g | Carbohydrates: approx 25 g | Fibre: approx 1 g | Protein: approx 5 g | Salt: approx 0.2 g

FRANCE

ESCARGOT

Escargot is a classic French delicacy featuring tender snails cooked in a rich garlic and herb butter. This air fryer version ensures perfectly cooked escargot with a deliciously crispy top.

Serves: 4 | Difficulty: Moderate | Prep Time: 15 minutes | Cook Time: 10 minutes | Total Time: 25 minutes

INGREDIENT LIST:

- 24 canned escargot (snails), drained and rinsed
- 100g unsalted butter, softened
- 4 cloves garlic, minced
- 2 tbsp fresh parsley, finely chopped
- 1 tbsp fresh chives, finely chopped
- 1 tbsp lemon juice
- Salt and pepper, to taste
- 24 small mushroom caps or escargot shells
- 4 tbsp breadcrumbs

PREPARATION:

1. **Prepare the Garlic Herb Butter:** In a bowl, mix the softened butter, minced garlic, chopped parsley, chopped chives, lemon juice, salt, and pepper until well combined.
2. **Stuff the Escargot:** Place each escargot into a mushroom cap or escargot shell. Top each with a generous amount of garlic herb butter, ensuring it is well covered.
3. **Preheat the Air Fryer:** Preheat the air fryer to 180 °C (360 °F).
4. **Air Fry the Escargot:** Arrange the stuffed escargot in a single layer in the air fryer basket. Sprinkle the tops with breadcrumbs. Cook for 8-10 minutes, or until the butter is bubbling and the tops are golden and crispy.
5. **Serve:** Transfer the escargot to a serving dish and serve immediately with crusty bread for dipping.

Tip: For an extra flavour boost, you can add a splash of white wine to the garlic herb butter mixture. Make sure to serve the escargot hot, as the butter will solidify as it cools.

ESTIMATED NUTRITIONAL TABLE PER 100G:

Calories: approx 250 kcal | Fat: approx 20 g | Carbohydrates: approx 10 g | Fibre: approx 1 g | Protein: approx 10 g | Salt: approx 0.4 g

COQ AU VIN

Coq au Vin is a traditional French dish featuring chicken braised in red wine with mushrooms, onions, and bacon. This air fryer version simplifies the process while maintaining the rich and complex flavours of the classic recipe.

Serves: 4 | Difficulty: Moderate | Prep Time: 20 minutes | Cook Time: 35 minutes | Total Time: 55 minutes

INGREDIENT LIST:

- 4 chicken thighs, bone-in and skin-on
- 200g bacon lardons
- 200g button mushrooms, halved
- 12 pearl onions, peeled
- 3 cloves garlic, minced
- 250ml red wine (Burgundy is traditional)
- 250ml chicken stock
- 2 tbsp tomato paste
- 2 tbsp plain flour
- 2 tbsp olive oil
- 1 tsp dried thyme
- 2 bay leaves
- Salt and pepper, to taste
- Fresh parsley, chopped, for garnish

PREPARATION:

1. **Preheat the Air Fryer:** Preheat the air fryer to 200 °C (390 °F).
2. **Cook the Bacon:** Place the bacon lardons in the air fryer basket and cook for 5 minutes until crispy. Remove and set aside.
3. **Brown the Chicken:** In a bowl, toss the chicken thighs with 1 tbsp of olive oil, salt, and pepper. Place the chicken thighs in the air fryer basket, skin side down, and cook for 10 minutes until browned. Remove and set aside.
4. **Cook the Vegetables:** Add the mushrooms, pearl onions, and minced garlic to the air fryer basket with the remaining 1 tbsp of olive oil. Cook for 5 minutes until softened.
5. **Make the Sauce:** In a bowl, whisk together the red wine, chicken stock, tomato paste, and plain flour until smooth. Pour this mixture over the vegetables in the air fryer basket. Add the browned chicken thighs, bacon lardons, dried thyme, and bay leaves.
6. **Braise the Chicken:** Reduce the air fryer temperature to 180 °C (360 °F). Cook for 20 minutes until the chicken is cooked through and the sauce has thickened. Stir halfway through to ensure even cooking.
7. **Serve:** Remove the bay leaves. Transfer the Coq au Vin to a serving dish and garnish with chopped fresh parsley. Serve hot.

Tip: For an authentic touch, serve Coq au Vin with crusty French bread or creamy mashed potatoes to soak up the rich sauce. Ensure the chicken is cooked to an internal temperature of at least 75 °C (165 °F) for safety.

ESTIMATED NUTRITIONAL TABLE PER 100G:

Calories: approx 200 kcal | Fat: approx 12 g | Carbohydrates: approx 6 g | Fibre: approx 1 g | Protein: approx 15 g | Salt: approx 0.6 g

RATATOUILLE

Ratatouille is a classic Provençal vegetable dish from France, featuring a medley of summer vegetables like aubergine, courgette, bell peppers, and tomatoes. This air fryer version ensures the vegetables are perfectly roasted, bringing out their natural sweetness and flavours.

Serves: 4 | Difficulty: Easy | Prep Time: 15 minutes | Cook Time: 25 minutes | Total Time: 40 minutes

INGREDIENT LIST:

- 1 large aubergine, diced
- 2 courgettes, sliced
- 1 red bell pepper, diced
- 1 yellow bell pepper, diced
- 1 red onion, chopped
- 3 tomatoes, chopped
- 3 cloves garlic, minced
- 3 tbsp olive oil
- 1 tsp dried thyme
- 1 tsp dried oregano
- Salt and pepper, to taste
- Fresh basil leaves, for garnish

PREPARATION:

1. **Preheat the Air Fryer:** Preheat the air fryer to 200 °C (390 °F).
2. **Prepare the Vegetables:** In a large bowl, combine the diced aubergine, sliced courgettes, diced bell peppers, chopped red onion, chopped tomatoes, and minced garlic. Drizzle with olive oil and sprinkle with dried thyme, dried oregano, salt, and pepper. Toss until the vegetables are evenly coated.
3. **Air Fry the Vegetables:** Place the vegetable mixture in the air fryer basket in a single layer. Cook for 20-25 minutes, shaking the basket halfway through, until the vegetables are tender and slightly caramelised.
4. **Serve:** Transfer the roasted vegetables to a serving dish and garnish with fresh basil leaves. Serve hot.

Tip: For added depth of flavour, you can add a splash of balsamic vinegar to the vegetables before roasting. Ratatouille can be served as a main dish with crusty bread or as a side dish with grilled meats or fish.

ESTIMATED NUTRITIONAL TABLE PER 100G:
Calories: approx 80 kcal | Fat: approx 5 g | Carbohydrates: approx 8 g | Fibre: approx 2 g | Protein: approx 1 g | Salt: approx 0.3 g

CRÈME BRÛLÉE

Crème Brûlée is a classic French dessert known for its creamy custard base topped with a contrasting layer of caramelised sugar. This air fryer version allows you to achieve a perfect custard with a crisp caramel top effortlessly.

Serves: 4 | Difficulty: Moderate | Prep Time: 15 minutes | Cook Time: 30 minutes | Total Time: 45 minutes (plus chilling time)

INGREDIENT LIST:

- 500ml double cream
- 1 vanilla pod, split and seeds scraped
- 5 large egg yolks
- 100g caster sugar (plus extra for caramelising)
- 1 tbsp light brown sugar

PREPARATION:

1. **Preheat the Air Fryer:** Preheat the air fryer to 150 °C (300 °F).
2. **Heat the Cream:** In a saucepan, combine the double cream and vanilla pod with seeds. Heat over medium heat until just simmering. Remove from heat and let it infuse for a few minutes.
3. **Prepare the Custard Base:** In a bowl, whisk the egg yolks with 100g caster sugar until pale and creamy. Gradually add the warm cream, whisking continuously. Remove the vanilla pod.
4. **Cook the Custard:** Pour the custard mixture into four ramekins. Place the ramekins in the air fryer basket. Cook for 25-30 minutes, or until the custard is set but still slightly wobbly in the centre.
5. **Chill the Custards:** Remove the ramekins from the air fryer and let them cool to room temperature. Then, refrigerate for at least 2 hours, or until thoroughly chilled.
6. **Caramelise the Sugar:** Just before serving, sprinkle a thin, even layer of caster sugar and light brown sugar on top of each custard. Use a kitchen blowtorch to caramelise the sugar until it forms a golden, crispy crust. Alternatively, you can place the ramekins under a preheated grill for a few minutes, watching closely to prevent burning.
7. **Serve:** Let the caramelised sugar cool for a minute to harden. Serve immediately.

Tip: For an extra touch of flavour, you can infuse the cream with a splash of your favourite liqueur before combining it with the egg yolk mixture. Ensure the custards are completely chilled before caramelising the sugar to achieve the perfect texture contrast.

ESTIMATED NUTRITIONAL TABLE PER 100G:

Calories: approx 300 kcal | Fat: approx 25 g | Carbohydrates: approx 18 g | Fibre: approx 0 g | Protein: approx 3 g | Salt: approx 0.1 g

SPAIN

PATATAS BRAVAS

Patatas Bravas is a popular Spanish tapas dish featuring crispy fried potatoes served with a spicy tomato sauce. This air fryer version ensures the potatoes are perfectly golden and crispy while reducing the oil content for a healthier twist.

Serves: 4 | Difficulty: Easy | Prep Time: 15 minutes | Cook Time: 20 minutes | Total Time: 35 minutes

INGREDIENT LIST:

- 600g potatoes, peeled and cut into bite-sized cubes
- 2 tbsp olive oil
- 1 tsp smoked paprika
- 1/2 tsp salt
- 1/2 tsp black pepper
- **For the Bravas Sauce:
- 1 tbsp olive oil
- 1 small onion, finely chopped
- 2 cloves garlic, minced
- 1 tsp smoked paprika
- 1/2 tsp hot paprika or chilli powder
- 1/2 tsp ground cumin
- 400g can chopped tomatoes
- 1 tbsp tomato paste
- 1 tsp sugar
- Salt and pepper, to taste

PREPARATION:

1. **Preheat the Air Fryer:** Preheat the air fryer to 200 °C (390 °F).
2. **Prepare the Potatoes:** In a large bowl, toss the potato cubes with 2 tbsp olive oil, smoked paprika, salt, and black pepper until evenly coated.
3. **Air Fry the Potatoes:** Place the seasoned potatoes in the air fryer basket in a single layer. Cook for 18-20 minutes, shaking the basket halfway through, until the potatoes are golden and crispy.
4. **Make the Bravas Sauce:** While the potatoes are cooking, heat 1 tbsp olive oil in a saucepan over medium heat. Add the finely chopped onion and minced garlic and cook until softened. Stir in the smoked paprika, hot paprika or chilli powder, and ground cumin, and cook for another minute. Add the chopped tomatoes, tomato paste, and sugar. Season with salt and pepper. Simmer the sauce for 10-15 minutes, until thickened.
5. **Blend the Sauce (Optional):** For a smoother sauce, you can blend the mixture using an immersion blender until smooth.
6. **Serve:** Transfer the crispy potatoes to a serving dish and spoon the bravas sauce over the top. Serve immediately.

Tip: For an extra touch of authenticity, garnish with a sprinkle of chopped fresh parsley. Patatas Bravas pairs wonderfully with other tapas dishes such as chorizo, gambas al ajillo (garlic shrimp), and a glass of sangria.

ESTIMATED NUTRITIONAL TABLE PER 100G:
Calories: approx 150 kcal | Fat: approx 6 g | Carbohydrates: approx 20 g | Fibre: approx 2 g | Protein: approx 2 g | Salt: approx 0.4 g

PAELLA

Paella is a traditional Spanish dish known for its vibrant flavours and beautiful presentation. This air fryer version features a delicious mix of seafood, chicken, and vegetables, all cooked together with saffron-infused rice.

Serves: 4 | Difficulty: Moderate | Prep Time: 20 minutes | Cook Time: 25 minutes | Total Time: 45 minutes

INGREDIENT LIST:

- 200g paella rice (Bomba or Arborio)
- 200g chicken breast, diced
- 200g mixed seafood (prawns, mussels, squid)
- 1 red bell pepper, diced
- 1 green bell pepper, diced
- 1 tomato, chopped
- 100g peas
- 1 onion, finely chopped
- 3 cloves garlic, minced
- 1 tsp smoked paprika
- 1/2 tsp saffron threads
- 750ml chicken stock
- 2 tbsp olive oil
- Salt and pepper, to taste
- Lemon wedges, for serving
- Fresh parsley, chopped, for garnish

PREPARATION:

1. **Prepare the Saffron Stock:** In a small bowl, steep the saffron threads in 2 tablespoons of warm water. Set aside.
2. **Cook the Chicken:** Preheat the air fryer to 200 °C (390 °F). Toss the diced chicken breast with 1 tablespoon of olive oil, salt, and pepper. Place in the air fryer basket and cook for 10 minutes, turning halfway through, until golden and cooked through. Remove and set aside.
3. **Cook the Vegetables:** In an air fryer-safe pan or dish, add the remaining olive oil, chopped onion, and minced garlic. Cook in the air fryer at 180 °C (360 °F) for 5 minutes until softened. Add the diced bell peppers, chopped tomato, and peas, and cook for an additional 5 minutes.
4. **Add the Rice and Spices:** Stir the paella rice into the vegetable mixture, ensuring it is well coated with the oil and juices. Add the smoked paprika and the saffron with its soaking water. Mix well.
5. **Add the Stock and Chicken:** Pour in the chicken stock and stir in the cooked chicken. Season with salt and pepper. Place the pan back in the air fryer and cook at 180 °C (360 °F) for 10 minutes.
6. **Add the Seafood:** After 10 minutes, gently stir the mixed seafood into the paella. Cook for an additional 10 minutes, or until the seafood is cooked through and the rice is tender.
7. **Serve:** Garnish the paella with fresh parsley and lemon wedges. Serve hot.

Tip: For an extra touch of flavour, you can add a splash of white wine to the stock mixture. Make sure to use a paella pan or any air fryer-safe dish that fits your air fryer basket comfortably.

ESTIMATED NUTRITIONAL TABLE PER 100G:

Calories: approx 160 kcal | Fat: approx 5 g | Carbohydrates: approx 18 g | Fibre: approx 1 g | Protein: approx 10 g | Salt: approx 0.6 g

GAMBAS AL AJILLO (GARLIC SHRIMP)

Gambas al Ajillo is a classic Spanish tapas dish featuring succulent shrimp sautéed with garlic and chilli. This air fryer version ensures the shrimp are perfectly cooked and infused with the rich flavours of garlic and olive oil.

Serves: 4 | Difficulty: Easy | Prep Time: 10 minutes | Cook Time: 8 minutes | Total Time: 18 minutes

INGREDIENT LIST:

- 500g large shrimp, peeled and deveined
- 4 cloves garlic, thinly sliced
- 1 red chilli, thinly sliced (or 1/2 tsp chilli flakes)
- 3 tbsp olive oil
- 1 tsp smoked paprika
- Salt and pepper, to taste
- Fresh parsley, chopped, for garnish
- Lemon wedges, for serving

PREPARATION:

1. **Preheat the Air Fryer:** Preheat the air fryer to 200 °C (390 °F).
2. **Prepare the Shrimp:** In a large bowl, toss the shrimp with the sliced garlic, sliced chilli, olive oil, smoked paprika, salt, and pepper until well coated.
3. **Air Fry the Shrimp:** Place the shrimp mixture in an air fryer-safe dish or directly in the air fryer basket in a single layer. Cook for 6-8 minutes, shaking the basket halfway through, until the shrimp are pink and cooked through.
4. **Serve:** Transfer the shrimp to a serving dish, sprinkle with chopped fresh parsley, and serve with lemon wedges on the side.

Tip: For an extra touch of flavour, you can add a splash of white wine or sherry to the shrimp before cooking. Serve Gambas al Ajillo with crusty bread to soak up the delicious garlic-infused olive oil.

ESTIMATED NUTRITIONAL TABLE PER 100G:
Calories: approx 150 kcal | Fat: approx 10 g | Carbohydrates: approx 1 g | Fibre: approx 0 g | Protein: approx 15 g | Salt: approx 0.7 g

FLAN

Flan, also known as crème caramel, is a beloved Spanish dessert featuring a smooth, creamy custard topped with a rich caramel sauce. This air fryer version ensures a perfect, silky texture with a beautifully caramelised top.

Serves: 4 | Difficulty: Moderate | Prep Time: 20 minutes | Cook Time: 30 minutes | Total Time: 50 minutes (plus chilling time)

INGREDIENT LIST:

For the Caramel:
- 150g granulated sugar
- 60ml water

For the Custard:
- 500ml whole milk
- 100g granulated sugar
- 4 large eggs
- 1 tsp vanilla extract

PREPARATION:

1. **Make the Caramel:** In a saucepan, combine the 150g of granulated sugar and 60ml of water. Heat over medium heat, swirling the pan occasionally until the sugar dissolves and turns a deep amber colour. Immediately pour the caramel into four individual ramekins, tilting each to coat the bottom evenly. Set aside to cool and harden.
2. **Prepare the Custard:** In a saucepan, heat the milk until just warm (do not boil). In a separate bowl, whisk together the eggs, 100g of granulated sugar, and vanilla extract until well combined. Gradually add the warm milk to the egg mixture, whisking constantly.
3. **Strain the Custard:** Pour the custard mixture through a fine mesh sieve into the caramel-coated ramekins, dividing it evenly.
4. **Preheat the Air Fryer:** Preheat the air fryer to 150 °C (300 °F).
5. **Air Fry the Flan:** Cover each ramekin with aluminium foil. Place the ramekins in the air fryer basket. Cook for 25-30 minutes, or until the custard is set but still slightly wobbly in the centre.
6. **Cool and Chill:** Remove the ramekins from the air fryer and let them cool to room temperature. Once cooled, refrigerate for at least 4 hours or overnight.
7. **Serve:** To serve, run a knife around the edge of each ramekin to loosen the flan. Invert onto a serving plate, allowing the caramel to drizzle over the top.

Tip: For an added flavour, you can infuse the milk with a cinnamon stick or a strip of lemon zest before warming it. Ensure the flan is fully chilled before serving to achieve the best texture.

ESTIMATED NUTRITIONAL TABLE PER 100G:
Calories: approx 180 kcal | Fat: approx 6 g | Carbohydrates: approx 27 g | Fibre: approx 0 g | Protein: approx 5 g | Salt: approx 0.1 g

GERMANY

PRETZELS

Pretzels are a traditional German snack known for their distinctive shape, chewy texture, and salty exterior. This air fryer version makes it easy to achieve perfectly baked pretzels at home with a golden, crisp crust.

Serves: 4 | Difficulty: Moderate | Prep Time: 20 minutes (plus rising time) | Cook Time: 10 minutes | Total Time: 30 minutes (plus rising time)

INGREDIENT LIST:

- 300g plain flour
- 1 tsp salt
- 1 tsp sugar
- 2 tsp instant yeast
- 200ml warm water
- 2 tbsp baking soda
- 1 egg, beaten (for egg wash)
- Coarse sea salt, for sprinkling

PREPARATION:

1. **Make the Dough:** In a large bowl, combine the plain flour, salt, sugar, and instant yeast. Gradually add the warm water, mixing until a dough forms. Knead the dough on a floured surface for about 5 minutes, until smooth and elastic.
2. **Let the Dough Rise:** Place the dough in a greased bowl, cover with a damp cloth, and let it rise in a warm place for about 1 hour, or until doubled in size.
3. **Preheat the Air Fryer:** Preheat the air fryer to 200 °C (390 °F).
4. **Shape the Pretzels:** Divide the dough into 8 equal pieces. Roll each piece into a long rope, about 45cm long. Shape each rope into a pretzel by forming a U-shape, crossing the ends over each other, and pressing them down onto the bottom of the U.
5. **Prepare the Baking Soda Solution:** In a large bowl, dissolve the baking soda in 500ml of hot water. Dip each pretzel into the baking soda solution for about 10 seconds, then place them on a parchment-lined tray to drain.
6. **Air Fry the Pretzels:** Brush each pretzel with the beaten egg and sprinkle with coarse sea salt. Place the pretzels in the air fryer basket in a single layer (you may need to do this in batches). Cook for 8-10 minutes, or until the pretzels are golden brown and cooked through.
7. **Serve:** Transfer the pretzels to a wire rack to cool slightly. Serve warm with mustard or cheese dip.

Tip: For a sweeter version, skip the coarse sea salt and sprinkle the pretzels with cinnamon sugar after brushing with the egg wash. Serve with a sweet dipping sauce for a delightful treat.

ESTIMATED NUTRITIONAL TABLE PER 100G:

Calories: approx 220 kcal | Fat: approx 2 g | Carbohydrates: approx 45 g | Fibre: approx 2 g | Protein: approx 6 g | Salt: approx 1.0 g

SCHNITZEL

Schnitzel is a classic German dish featuring thinly pounded meat, breaded and fried to a crispy golden brown. This air fryer version ensures a healthier take on the traditional schnitzel while maintaining its delicious crunch and tenderness.

Serves: 4 | Difficulty: Moderate | Prep Time: 15 minutes | Cook Time: 15 minutes | Total Time: 30 minutes

INGREDIENT LIST:

- 4 boneless pork chops or chicken breasts, pounded to 1/2-inch thickness
- 100g plain flour
- 2 large eggs, beaten
- 100g breadcrumbs
- 50g grated Parmesan cheese
- 1 tsp salt
- 1/2 tsp black pepper
- 1 tsp paprika
- 2 tbsp olive oil
- Lemon wedges, for serving
- Fresh parsley, chopped, for garnish

PREPARATION:

1. **Preheat the Air Fryer:** Preheat the air fryer to 200 °C (390 °F).
2. **Prepare the Breading Stations:** Set up three shallow bowls: one with plain flour, one with beaten eggs, and one with a mixture of breadcrumbs, grated Parmesan cheese, salt, black pepper, and paprika.
3. **Bread the Meat:** Dredge each piece of meat in the flour, shaking off any excess. Dip in the beaten eggs, then coat with the breadcrumb mixture, pressing lightly to adhere.
4. **Air Fry the Schnitzel:** Lightly brush or spray both sides of the breaded meat with olive oil. Place the schnitzel in the air fryer basket in a single layer (you may need to do this in batches). Cook for 10-12 minutes, turning halfway through, until the schnitzel is golden brown and cooked through.
5. **Serve:** Transfer the schnitzel to a serving plate. Garnish with chopped fresh parsley and serve with lemon wedges on the side.

Tip: For an extra crispy coating, you can double dip the meat by repeating the egg and breadcrumb steps. Serve the schnitzel with a side of German potato salad or a fresh green salad for a complete meal.

ESTIMATED NUTRITIONAL TABLE PER 100G:
Calories: approx 250 kcal | Fat: approx 12 g | Carbohydrates: approx 15 g | Fibre: approx 1 g | Protein: approx 20 g | Salt: approx 0.8 g

SAUERKRAUT BALLS

Sauerkraut Balls are a tasty German appetiser featuring a savoury mixture of sauerkraut, sausage, and cream cheese, breaded and fried to perfection. This air fryer version ensures a crispy exterior and a delicious, tangy filling.

Serves: 4 | Difficulty: Moderate | Prep Time: 20 minutes | Cook Time: 12 minutes | Total Time: 32 minutes

INGREDIENT LIST:

- 200g sauerkraut, well-drained and finely chopped
- 150g ground sausage (pork or beef)
- 100g cream cheese, softened
- 1 small onion, finely chopped
- 2 cloves garlic, minced
- 1 tsp mustard
- 1/2 tsp paprika
- 100g plain flour
- 2 large eggs, beaten
- 100g breadcrumbs
- Salt and pepper, to taste
- 2 tbsp vegetable oil

PREPARATION:

1. **Cook the Sausage:** In a frying pan over medium heat, cook the ground sausage until browned and fully cooked. Remove from heat and let it cool.
2. **Combine the Filling:** In a large bowl, mix the cooked sausage, chopped sauerkraut, cream cheese, chopped onion, minced garlic, mustard, paprika, salt, and pepper until well combined.
3. **Shape the Balls:** Roll the mixture into small balls, about the size of a walnut. Place them on a tray and refrigerate for 30 minutes to firm up.
4. **Preheat the Air Fryer:** Preheat the air fryer to 180 °C (360 °F).
5. **Bread the Balls:** Set up three shallow bowls: one with plain flour, one with beaten eggs, and one with breadcrumbs. Roll each sauerkraut ball in the flour, then dip in the beaten eggs, and coat with breadcrumbs.
6. **Air Fry the Sauerkraut Balls:** Lightly spray the sauerkraut balls with vegetable oil. Place them in the air fryer basket in a single layer, ensuring they do not touch. Cook for 10-12 minutes, turning halfway through, until golden brown and crispy.
7. **Serve:** Transfer the sauerkraut balls to a serving plate and serve hot with mustard or your favourite dipping sauce.

Tip: For added flavour, you can mix some grated cheese into the filling. Ensure the sauerkraut is well-drained to prevent the mixture from becoming too wet.

ESTIMATED NUTRITIONAL TABLE PER 100G:

Calories: approx 250 kcal | Fat: approx 18 g | Carbohydrates: approx 15 g | Fibre: approx 2 g | Protein: approx 8 g | Salt: approx 1.2 g

BLACK FOREST CAKE

Black Forest Cake, or Schwarzwälder Kirschtorte, is a classic German dessert featuring layers of rich chocolate cake, whipped cream, and cherries. This air fryer version ensures a moist and delicious cake with all the traditional flavours.

Serves: 8 | Difficulty: Moderate | Prep Time: 30 minutes | Cook Time: 25 minutes | Total Time: 55 minutes

INGREDIENT LIST:

For the Cake:
- 150g plain flour
- 50g cocoa powder
- 1 tsp baking powder
- 1/2 tsp bicarbonate of soda
- 1/4 tsp salt
- 200g granulated sugar
- 2 large eggs
- 120ml buttermilk
- 120ml vegetable oil
- 1 tsp vanilla extract
- 120ml hot water

For the Filling and Topping:
- 400ml double cream
- 50g icing sugar
- 1 tsp vanilla extract
- 300g canned sour cherries, drained and juice reserved
- 2 tbsp cherry brandy (Kirsch)
- 50g dark chocolate, grated

PREPARATION:

1. **Preheat the Air Fryer:** Preheat the air fryer to 160 °C (320 °F). Grease and line two 18cm (7-inch) round cake tins.
2. **Make the Cake Batter:** In a large bowl, sift together the plain flour, cocoa powder, baking powder, bicarbonate of soda, and salt. In another bowl, whisk together the granulated sugar, eggs, buttermilk, vegetable oil, and vanilla extract. Gradually add the dry ingredients to the wet ingredients, mixing until just combined. Stir in the hot water until smooth.
3. **Bake the Cakes:** Divide the batter evenly between the prepared cake tins. Place the tins in the air fryer basket. Cook for 20-25 minutes, or until a skewer inserted into the centre comes out clean. Let the cakes cool in the tins for 10 minutes, then transfer to a wire rack to cool completely.
4. **Prepare the Filling:** In a bowl, whip the double cream, icing sugar, and vanilla extract until stiff peaks form.
5. **Assemble the Cake:** Once the cakes are completely cool, level the tops if necessary. Place one cake layer on a serving plate. Brush with half of the reserved cherry juice mixed with the cherry brandy. Spread a layer of whipped cream over the cake, then scatter half of the drained sour cherries on top. Place the second cake layer on top and repeat the process with the remaining cherry juice, whipped cream, and cherries.
6. **Decorate the Cake:** Cover the entire cake with the remaining whipped cream. Sprinkle the grated dark chocolate over the top and sides of the cake.
7. **Serve:** Chill the cake in the refrigerator for at least 1 hour before serving to allow the flavours to meld together.

Tip: For an extra indulgent touch, add a layer of chocolate ganache between the cake layers. Ensure the cakes are completely cool before assembling to prevent the whipped cream from melting.

ESTIMATED NUTRITIONAL TABLE PER 100G:
Calories: approx 320 kcal | Fat: approx 20 g | Carbohydrates: approx 30 g | Fibre: approx 2 g | Protein: approx 5 g | Salt: approx 0.3 g

UNITED KINGDOM

SCOTCH EGGS

Scotch Eggs are a quintessential British snack, combining a soft-boiled egg wrapped in seasoned sausage meat, coated in breadcrumbs, and air-fried to crispy perfection. They are often enjoyed as a picnic treat or a substantial snack.

Serves: 4 | Difficulty: Moderate | Prep Time: 20 minutes | Cook Time: 12 minutes | Total Time: 32 minutes

INGREDIENT LIST:

- 4 large eggs
- 450g sausage meat
- 1 tsp English mustard
- 1 tsp dried thyme
- 1/2 tsp salt
- 1/2 tsp black pepper
- 50g plain flour
- 1 large egg, beaten
- 100g breadcrumbs
- Cooking spray

PREPARATION:

1. **Boil the Eggs:** Place 4 large eggs in a saucepan and cover with water. Bring to a boil and cook for 4-5 minutes for soft-boiled or 8 minutes for hard-boiled. Transfer to a bowl of ice water to cool, then peel.
2. **Prepare the Sausage Meat:** In a large bowl, combine the sausage meat, English mustard, dried thyme, salt, and black pepper. Divide into 4 equal portions.
3. **Wrap the Eggs:** Flatten each portion of sausage meat into a patty. Place an egg in the centre of each patty and wrap the sausage meat around the egg, sealing completely.
4. **Coat the Eggs:** Place the flour, beaten egg, and breadcrumbs into separate shallow bowls. Roll each sausage-wrapped egg in the flour, then dip in the beaten egg, and finally coat with breadcrumbs. Press gently to ensure the breadcrumbs adhere.
5. **Air Fry:** Preheat the air fryer to 200 °C (390 °F). Lightly spray the coated eggs with cooking spray. Place the Scotch eggs in the air fryer basket, ensuring they are not touching. Air fry for 10-12 minutes, turning halfway through, until the sausage is cooked and the coating is golden and crispy.
6. **Serve:** Allow the Scotch eggs to cool slightly before slicing in half. Serve warm or at room temperature.

Tip: For a healthier version, use lean sausage meat and wholemeal breadcrumbs.

ESTIMATED NUTRITIONAL TABLE PER 100G:

Calories: approx 250 kcal | Fat: approx 16 g | Carbohydrates: approx 12 g | Fibre: approx 1 g | Protein: approx 15 g | Salt: approx 1.2 g

FISH AND CHIPS

Fish and Chips is a classic British dish, featuring crispy battered fish and golden chips. This air-fryer version retains all the traditional flavours and textures while being healthier and less greasy.

Serves: 4 | Difficulty: Moderate | Prep Time: 20 minutes |
Cook Time: 25 minutes | Total Time: 45 minutes

INGREDIENT LIST:

- 4 large potatoes, peeled and cut into chips
- 2 tbsp vegetable oil
- Salt, to taste
- 4 skinless cod fillets (about 150g each)
- 100g plain flour
- 1/2 tsp baking powder
- 150ml cold sparkling water
- 1 egg
- 1/2 tsp salt
- 1/2 tsp black pepper
- 1 lemon, cut into wedges

PREPARATION:

1. **Prepare the Chips:** Soak the cut potatoes in cold water for 30 minutes to remove excess starch. Drain and pat dry with a clean tea towel.
2. **Season and Cook the Chips:** Preheat the air fryer to 180 °C (360 °F). Toss the potatoes with 1 tbsp of vegetable oil and a pinch of salt. Place the chips in the air fryer basket in a single layer. Air fry for 15-20 minutes, shaking the basket halfway through, until golden and crispy. Remove and keep warm.
3. **Prepare the Batter:** In a bowl, mix the flour, baking powder, salt, and black pepper. In another bowl, beat the egg and combine with cold sparkling water. Gradually whisk the wet mixture into the dry ingredients until smooth.
4. **Coat the Fish:** Pat the cod fillets dry with kitchen paper. Dust each fillet lightly with flour, then dip into the batter, allowing any excess to drip off.
5. **Air Fry the Fish:** Increase the air fryer temperature to 200 °C (390 °F). Spray the basket with a little vegetable oil to prevent sticking. Place the battered fillets in the air fryer basket in a single layer. Cook for 10-12 minutes, turning halfway through, until the batter is golden and the fish is cooked through.
6. **Serve:** Serve the fish and chips immediately with lemon wedges on the side.

Tip: For an extra crispy finish, spray the battered fish lightly with oil before cooking. Serve with mushy peas and tartar sauce for a traditional touch.

ESTIMATED NUTRITIONAL TABLE PER 100G:
Calories: approx 190 kcal | Fat: approx 6 g | Carbohydrates: approx 23 g |
Fibre: approx 2 g | Protein: approx 10 g | Salt: approx 0.5 g

ROAST POTATOES

Crispy on the outside and fluffy on the inside, roast potatoes are a staple of British Sunday lunches. This air fryer version delivers perfect roasties with less oil and a shorter cooking time.

Serves: 4 | Difficulty: Easy | Prep Time: 10 minutes | Cook Time: 25 minutes | Total Time: 35 minutes

INGREDIENT LIST:

- 1 kg Maris Piper or King Edward potatoes, peeled and cut into chunks
- 2 tbsp vegetable oil
- 1 tsp salt
- 1/2 tsp black pepper
- 1 tsp dried rosemary or thyme (optional)

PREPARATION:

1. **Preheat the Air Fryer:** Preheat the air fryer to 200 °C (390 °F).
2. **Prepare the Potatoes:** Place the potato chunks in a pot of cold water. Bring to a boil and cook for 5 minutes. Drain well and let them steam dry for a few minutes.
3. **Season the Potatoes:** In a large bowl, toss the potatoes with vegetable oil, salt, black pepper, and dried herbs if using. Shake the bowl to roughen up the edges of the potatoes for extra crispiness.
4. **Air Fry:** Place the potatoes in the air fryer basket in a single layer. Cook for 25 minutes, shaking the basket every 10 minutes to ensure even cooking. The potatoes should be golden and crispy.
5. **Serve:** Transfer the roast potatoes to a serving dish and serve immediately.

Tip: For an extra crunchy texture, sprinkle a small amount of semolina or cornmeal on the potatoes after parboiling and before air frying.

ESTIMATED NUTRITIONAL TABLE PER 100G:
Calories: approx 110 kcal | Fat: approx 3 g | Carbohydrates: approx 19 g | Fibre: approx 2 g | Protein: approx 2 g | Salt: approx 0.3 g

STICKY TOFFEE PUDDING

Sticky Toffee Pudding is a beloved British dessert, featuring a moist sponge cake made with dates, drenched in a rich toffee sauce. This air fryer version offers a quicker and equally delicious way to enjoy this classic treat.

Serves: 4 | Difficulty: Moderate | Prep Time: 20 minutes | Cook Time: 20 minutes | Total Time: 40 minutes

INGREDIENT LIST:

For the Pudding:
- 150g dates, pitted and chopped
- 175ml boiling water
- 1 tsp bicarbonate of soda
- 50g unsalted butter, softened
- 75g dark brown sugar
- 2 large eggs
- 1 tsp vanilla extract
- 175g self-raising flour

For the Toffee Sauce:
- 100g dark brown sugar
- 100g unsalted butter
- 150ml double cream
- 1 tsp vanilla extract

PREPARATION:

1. **Prepare the Dates:** Place the chopped dates in a bowl and pour over the boiling water. Stir in the bicarbonate of soda and let it sit for 10 minutes to soften.
2. **Make the Pudding Batter:** In a large bowl, cream together the butter and dark brown sugar until light and fluffy. Beat in the eggs one at a time, then add the vanilla extract. Fold in the flour, followed by the softened date mixture, until well combined.
3. **Air Fry the Pudding:** Preheat the air fryer to 160 °C (320 °F). Grease four small pudding moulds or ramekins and divide the batter evenly among them. Place the moulds in the air fryer basket. Cook for 18-20 minutes, or until a skewer inserted into the centre comes out clean.
4. **Make the Toffee Sauce:** While the puddings are cooking, prepare the toffee sauce. In a saucepan over medium heat, melt the butter and dark brown sugar together. Stir in the double cream and vanilla extract, and bring to a simmer. Cook for 3-5 minutes, until the sauce thickens slightly.
5. **Serve:** Once the puddings are cooked, remove them from the air fryer and allow them to cool for a few minutes. Turn them out onto serving plates and pour the warm toffee sauce over each pudding. Serve immediately.

Tip: For an extra indulgent touch, serve with a scoop of vanilla ice cream or a dollop of clotted cream.

ESTIMATED NUTRITIONAL TABLE PER 100G:

Calories: approx 300 kcal | Fat: approx 15 g | Carbohydrates: approx 40 g | Fibre: approx 2 g | Protein: approx 3 g | Salt: approx 0.3 g

CHAPTER 4: ASIA

CHINA

SPRING ROLLS

Spring Rolls are a popular Chinese appetiser filled with a mixture of vegetables and sometimes meat, wrapped in a thin pastry and fried until crispy. This air fryer version ensures a crunchy exterior and a deliciously savoury filling.

Serves: 4 | Difficulty: Moderate | Prep Time: 20 minutes | Cook Time: 12 minutes | Total Time: 32 minutes

INGREDIENT LIST:

- 200g cabbage, finely shredded
- 1 large carrot, grated
- 100g bean sprouts
- 2 spring onions, finely sliced
- 2 cloves garlic, minced
- 1 tbsp soy sauce
- 1 tbsp oyster sauce
- 1 tsp sesame oil
- 1 tsp grated ginger
- 1/2 tsp white pepper
- 12 spring roll wrappers
- 1 tbsp vegetable oil (for brushing)
- Sweet chilli sauce, for serving

PREPARATION:

1. **Prepare the Filling:** In a large bowl, combine the shredded cabbage, grated carrot, bean sprouts, sliced spring onions, and minced garlic. Add the soy sauce, oyster sauce, sesame oil, grated ginger, and white pepper. Mix well until all ingredients are evenly distributed.
2. **Assemble the Spring Rolls:** Place a spring roll wrapper on a clean surface with one corner pointing towards you. Spoon about 2 tablespoons of the filling onto the lower part of the wrapper. Fold the bottom corner over the filling, then fold in the sides and roll up tightly. Brush the edge with a little water to seal. Repeat with the remaining wrappers and filling.
3. **Preheat the Air Fryer:** Preheat the air fryer to 180 °C (360 °F).
4. **Air Fry the Spring Rolls:** Lightly brush the spring rolls with vegetable oil on all sides. Place them in the air fryer basket in a single layer, ensuring they do not touch. Cook for 10-12 minutes, turning halfway through, until golden brown and crispy.
5. **Serve:** Transfer the spring rolls to a serving plate and serve hot with sweet chilli sauce for dipping.

Tip: For a variation, you can add cooked chicken, shrimp, or pork to the filling. Ensure the spring rolls are tightly rolled to prevent them from bursting open during cooking.

ESTIMATED NUTRITIONAL TABLE PER 100G:
Calories: approx 150 kcal | Fat: approx 5 g | Carbohydrates: approx 20 g | Fibre: approx 2 g | Protein: approx 3 g | Salt: approx 0.8 g

SWEET AND SOUR CHICKEN

Sweet and Sour Chicken is a popular Chinese dish known for its crispy chicken pieces coated in a tangy, sweet, and slightly sour sauce. This air fryer version ensures a healthier alternative with the same delicious flavours.

Serves: 4 | Difficulty: Moderate | Prep Time: 20 minutes | Cook Time: 15 minutes | Total Time: 35 minutes

INGREDIENT LIST:

For the Chicken:
- 500g chicken breast, cut into bite-sized pieces
- 100g plain flour
- 2 large eggs, beaten
- 100g breadcrumbs
- 1 tsp salt
- 1/2 tsp black pepper
- 2 tbsp vegetable oil (for brushing)

For the Sauce:
- 2 tbsp vegetable oil
- 1 red bell pepper, diced
- 1 green bell pepper, diced
- 1 onion, diced
- 1 large carrot, sliced
- 2 cloves garlic, minced
- 200g pineapple chunks (canned, drained)
- 3 tbsp ketchup
- 2 tbsp soy sauce
- 3 tbsp rice vinegar
- 3 tbsp brown sugar
- 1 tbsp cornflour mixed with 2 tbsp water (for thickening)

PREPARATION:
1. **Prepare the Chicken:** Preheat the air fryer to 200 °C (390 °F). In separate **shallow** bowls, place the flour, beaten eggs, and breadcrumbs. Season the breadcrumbs with salt and black pepper. Dredge each piece of chicken in the flour, dip in the beaten eggs, and coat with breadcrumbs. Lightly brush the chicken pieces with vegetable oil.
2. **Air Fry the Chicken:** Place the breaded chicken pieces in the air fryer basket in a single layer. Cook for 12-15 minutes, turning halfway through, until the chicken is golden brown and cooked through.
3. **Make the Sauce:** While the chicken is cooking, heat 2 tbsp of vegetable oil in a large pan over medium heat. Add the diced red and green bell peppers, onion, carrot, and minced garlic. Cook for 5 minutes until the vegetables are tender. Add the pineapple chunks, ketchup, soy sauce, rice vinegar, and brown sugar. Stir well and bring to a simmer.
4. **Thicken the Sauce:** Stir in the cornflour mixture and cook for another 2 minutes until the sauce thickens.
5. **Combine and Serve:** Add the cooked chicken pieces to the sauce and toss to coat evenly. Serve the sweet and sour chicken immediately over steamed rice or noodles.

Tip: For extra crunch, you can double-coat the chicken pieces by repeating the flour, egg, and breadcrumb steps. Ensure the sauce is thick enough to coat the chicken well without becoming too watery.

ESTIMATED NUTRITIONAL TABLE PER 100G:
Calories: approx 180 kcal | Fat: approx 8 g | Carbohydrates: approx 18 g | Fibre: approx 2 g | Protein: approx 9 g | Salt: approx 1.0 g

FRIED RICE

Fried Rice is a versatile and popular Chinese dish made with cooked rice stir-fried with vegetables, eggs, and a savoury sauce. This air fryer version ensures a perfectly cooked and flavourful dish with minimal effort.

Serves: 4 | Difficulty: Easy | Prep Time: 15 minutes | Cook Time: 10 minutes | Total Time: 25 minutes

INGREDIENT LIST:

- 300g cooked and cooled jasmine rice (preferably day-old)
- 2 tbsp vegetable oil
- 2 large eggs, beaten
- 1 onion, finely chopped
- 2 cloves garlic, minced
- 1 carrot, diced
- 100g frozen peas
- 3 spring onions, sliced
- 3 tbsp soy sauce
- 1 tbsp oyster sauce
- 1 tsp sesame oil
- Salt and pepper, to taste

PREPARATION:

1. **Preheat the Air Fryer:** Preheat the air fryer to 200 °C (390 °F).
2. **Prepare the Egg:** Lightly grease an air fryer-safe dish or pan with 1 tbsp of vegetable oil. Pour the beaten eggs into the dish and cook in the air fryer for 3-4 minutes until set. Remove and cut into small pieces. Set aside.
3. **Cook the Vegetables:** In the same air fryer-safe dish, add the remaining 1 tbsp of vegetable oil. Add the chopped onion, minced garlic, diced carrot, and frozen peas. Cook for 5 minutes until the vegetables are tender.
4. **Combine Ingredients:** Add the cooked and cooled rice to the dish with the vegetables. Add the cooked egg pieces, sliced spring onions, soy sauce, oyster sauce, and sesame oil. Toss everything together until well combined.
5. **Air Fry the Fried Rice:** Return the dish to the air fryer and cook for an additional 5 minutes, stirring halfway through, until the rice is heated through and slightly crispy on the edges.
6. **Serve:** Season the fried rice with salt and pepper to taste. Serve hot as a main dish or a side.

Tip: For added protein, you can include cooked chicken, shrimp, or tofu in the fried rice. Make sure the rice is properly cooled before frying to prevent it from becoming mushy.

ESTIMATED NUTRITIONAL TABLE PER 100G:
Calories: approx 150 kcal | Fat: approx 6 g | Carbohydrates: approx 20 g | Fibre: approx 2 g | Protein: approx 4 g | Salt: approx 0.8 g

SESAME BALLS

Sesame Balls, also known as Jian Dui, are a popular Chinese dessert featuring a chewy glutinous rice dough filled with sweet red bean paste, coated in sesame seeds, and fried until golden. This air fryer version offers a healthier alternative while maintaining the delicious taste and texture.

Serves: 4 | Difficulty: Moderate | Prep Time: 20 minutes | Cook Time: 15 minutes | Total Time: 35 minutes

INGREDIENT LIST:

- 200g glutinous rice flour
- 100g caster sugar
- 120ml water
- 100g red bean paste
- 100g white sesame seeds
- 2 tbsp vegetable oil (for brushing)

PREPARATION:

1. **Make the Dough:** In a large bowl, mix the glutinous rice flour and caster sugar. Gradually add water, stirring until a smooth dough forms. The dough should be soft but not sticky.
2. **Divide and Fill the Dough:** Divide the dough into 12 equal pieces. Flatten each piece into a small disc and place a teaspoon of red bean paste in the centre. Wrap the dough around the filling, rolling it into a smooth ball.
3. **Coat with Sesame Seeds:** Roll each ball in a bowl of sesame seeds, pressing gently to ensure the seeds adhere to the surface.
4. **Preheat the Air Fryer:** Preheat the air fryer to 180 °C (360 °F).
5. **Air Fry the Sesame Balls:** Lightly brush each sesame ball with vegetable oil. Place them in the air fryer basket in a single layer, ensuring they do not touch. Cook for 12-15 minutes, shaking the basket halfway through, until the sesame balls are golden and crispy.
6. **Serve:** Allow the sesame balls to cool slightly before serving. Enjoy warm or at room temperature.

Tip: For an extra touch of flavour, you can add a few drops of vanilla extract to the dough. Ensure the dough is sealed tightly around the filling to prevent any leakage during cooking.

ESTIMATED NUTRITIONAL TABLE PER 100G:
Calories: approx 200 kcal | Fat: approx 7 g | Carbohydrates: approx 30 g | Fibre: approx 2 g | Protein: approx 4 g | Salt: approx 0.1 g

JAPAN

GYOZA

Gyoza are Japanese dumplings filled with a savoury mixture of meat and vegetables, traditionally pan-fried until crispy and steamed until tender. This air fryer version ensures a perfect balance of crispy bottoms and juicy filling.

Serves: 4 | Difficulty: Moderate | Prep Time: 30 minutes | Cook Time: 12 minutes | Total Time: 42 minutes

INGREDIENT LIST:

- 200g ground pork
- 100g cabbage, finely shredded
- 1 small carrot, grated
- 2 spring onions, finely chopped
- 2 cloves garlic, minced
- 1 tsp grated ginger
- 1 tbsp soy sauce
- 1 tbsp sake (optional)
- 1 tsp sesame oil
- 1/2 tsp salt
- 1/4 tsp black pepper
- 24 gyoza wrappers
- 2 tbsp vegetable oil (for brushing)
- Dipping sauce (soy sauce, rice vinegar, and a few drops of sesame oil)

PREPARATION:

1. **Make the Filling:** In a large bowl, combine the ground pork, shredded cabbage, grated carrot, chopped spring onions, minced garlic, grated ginger, soy sauce, sake (if using), sesame oil, salt, and black pepper. Mix until well combined.
2. **Assemble the Gyoza:** Place a gyoza wrapper in the palm of your hand. Spoon about 1 teaspoon of the filling into the centre of the wrapper. Moisten the edges of the wrapper with water, fold it in half, and press the edges together to seal, pleating the edges if desired. Repeat with the remaining wrappers and filling.
3. **Preheat the Air Fryer:** Preheat the air fryer to 180 °C (360 °F).
4. **Air Fry the Gyoza:** Lightly brush the gyoza with vegetable oil on both sides. Arrange them in a single layer in the air fryer basket, ensuring they do not touch. Cook for 10-12 minutes, turning halfway through, until the gyoza are golden and crispy.
5. **Serve:** Serve the gyoza hot with a dipping sauce made from soy sauce, rice vinegar, and a few drops of sesame oil.

Tip: For added flavour, you can add a pinch of chilli flakes or a dash of chilli oil to the dipping sauce. Ensure the gyoza are tightly sealed to prevent the filling from leaking during cooking.

ESTIMATED NUTRITIONAL TABLE PER 100G:
Calories: approx 180 kcal | Fat: approx 9 g | Carbohydrates: approx 15 g | Fibre: approx 1 g | Protein: approx 8 g | Salt: approx 1.0 g

TERIYAKI SALMON

Teriyaki Salmon is a delicious Japanese dish featuring salmon fillets glazed with a sweet and savoury teriyaki sauce. This air fryer version ensures perfectly cooked, tender salmon with a caramelised teriyaki glaze.

Serves: 4 | Difficulty: Easy | Prep Time: 10 minutes | Cook Time: 12 minutes | Total Time: 22 minutes

INGREDIENT LIST:

- 4 salmon fillets (about 150g each)
- 60ml soy sauce
- 60ml mirin
- 60ml sake (or water)
- 2 tbsp brown sugar
- 1 clove garlic, minced
- 1 tsp grated ginger
- 1 tbsp vegetable oil
- 1 tsp sesame seeds (optional)
- Spring onions, finely sliced, for garnish

PREPARATION:

1. **Make the Teriyaki Sauce:** In a small saucepan, combine the soy sauce, mirin, sake (or water), brown sugar, minced garlic, and grated ginger. Bring to a boil over medium heat, then reduce the heat and simmer for 5 minutes until slightly thickened. Remove from heat and let cool.
2. **Marinate the Salmon:** Place the salmon fillets in a shallow dish. Pour half of the teriyaki sauce over the salmon, reserving the other half for glazing. Marinate for at least 10 minutes.
3. **Preheat the Air Fryer:** Preheat the air fryer to 180 °C (360 °F).
4. **Cook the Salmon:** Lightly brush the air fryer basket with vegetable oil to prevent sticking. Place the marinated salmon fillets in the basket, skin side down. Cook for 10-12 minutes, basting with the reserved teriyaki sauce halfway through, until the salmon is cooked through and caramelised on top.
5. **Serve:** Transfer the salmon to a serving plate. Sprinkle with sesame seeds and garnish with finely sliced spring onions. Serve with steamed rice and vegetables.

Tip: For extra flavour, you can add a pinch of chilli flakes to the teriyaki sauce. Ensure the salmon fillets are of even thickness to ensure even cooking.

ESTIMATED NUTRITIONAL TABLE PER 100G:
Calories: approx 200 kcal | Fat: approx 10 g | Carbohydrates: approx 8 g | Fibre: approx 0 g | Protein: approx 20 g | Salt: approx 1.2 g

TEMPURA VEGETABLES

Tempura Vegetables are a classic Japanese dish featuring a variety of vegetables lightly battered and fried to a crispy perfection. This air fryer version ensures a healthier take with the same delicate crunch and flavour.

Serves: 4 | Difficulty: Moderate | Prep Time: 20 minutes | Cook Time: 15 minutes | Total Time: 35 minutes

INGREDIENT LIST:

- 1 small aubergine, sliced into thin rounds
- 1 courgette, sliced into thin rounds
- 1 sweet potato, peeled and thinly sliced
- 1 red bell pepper, cut into strips
- 100g broccoli florets
- 100g plain flour
- 50g cornflour
- 1/2 tsp baking powder
- 200ml ice-cold sparkling water
- 1 egg, beaten
- 1/2 tsp salt
- 2 tbsp vegetable oil (for brushing)
- Soy sauce or tempura dipping sauce, for serving

PREPARATION:

1. **Prepare the Vegetables:** Cut the vegetables into uniform, bite-sized pieces. Pat them dry with kitchen paper to remove excess moisture.
2. **Make the Batter:** In a large bowl, mix the plain flour, cornflour, and baking powder. Add the ice-cold sparkling water, beaten egg, and salt, stirring gently until just combined. Be careful not to overmix; the batter should be slightly lumpy.
3. **Preheat the Air Fryer:** Preheat the air fryer to 180 °C (360 °F).
4. **Coat the Vegetables:** Dip each vegetable piece into the batter, letting any excess drip off. Place the battered vegetables on a plate.
5. **Air Fry the Tempura:** Lightly brush or spray the air fryer basket with vegetable oil. Place the battered vegetables in the basket in a single layer, ensuring they do not touch. Lightly brush the tops with vegetable oil. Cook for 12-15 minutes, turning halfway through, until the vegetables are golden and crispy.
6. **Serve:** Transfer the tempura vegetables to a serving plate. Serve immediately with soy sauce or tempura dipping sauce.

Tip: For the crispiest tempura, ensure the batter and the vegetables are very cold before frying. You can also add a pinch of turmeric to the batter for a slight golden colour and extra flavour.

ESTIMATED NUTRITIONAL TABLE PER 100G:
Calories: approx 120 kcal | Fat: approx 5 g | Carbohydrates: approx 15 g | Fibre: approx 2 g | Protein: approx 2 g | Salt: approx 0.5 g

MOCHI

Mochi is a traditional Japanese rice cake made from glutinous rice flour, known for its chewy texture. This air fryer version simplifies the process, resulting in deliciously soft and chewy mochi that can be enjoyed plain or filled with sweet fillings like red bean paste.

Serves: 4 | Difficulty: Moderate | Prep Time: 15 minutes | Cook Time: 10 minutes | Total Time: 25 minutes

INGREDIENT LIST:

- 200g glutinous rice flour
- 100g granulated sugar
- 200ml water
- Cornflour, for dusting
- Sweet red bean paste or other fillings (optional)

PREPARATION:

1. **Make the Dough:** In a large microwave-safe bowl, mix the glutinous rice flour and granulated sugar. Gradually add the water, stirring until smooth and well combined.
2. **Cook the Dough:** Cover the bowl with cling film, leaving a small gap for steam to escape. Microwave on high for 2 minutes, then stir the mixture. Microwave for another 1-2 minutes until the dough is thick and slightly translucent.
3. **Shape the Mochi:** Dust a clean work surface and your hands with cornflour. Transfer the cooked mochi dough to the work surface and let it cool slightly. Knead the dough a few times until smooth. Divide the dough into small portions (about 12-15 pieces).
4. **Fill the Mochi (Optional):** If using a filling, flatten each portion of dough into a small disc, place a small spoonful of red bean paste or other fillings in the centre, and fold the dough over the filling, pinching the edges to seal. Roll the filled mochi into balls.
5. **Preheat the Air Fryer:** Preheat the air fryer to 180 °C (360 °F).
6. **Air Fry the Mochi:** Place the mochi balls in the air fryer basket, ensuring they do not touch. Cook for 5-7 minutes, or until slightly crispy on the outside.
7. **Serve:** Allow the mochi to cool slightly before serving. Enjoy them warm or at room temperature.

Tip: For a variation, you can add a few drops of food colouring to the dough before cooking to create colourful mochi. Mochi is best enjoyed fresh but can be stored in an airtight container for up to a day.

ESTIMATED NUTRITIONAL TABLE PER 100G:

Calories: approx 180 kcal | Fat: approx 0 g | Carbohydrates: approx 42 g | Fibre: approx 0 g | Protein: approx 3 g | Salt: approx 0 g

INDIA

SAMOSAS

Samosas are a popular Indian snack featuring a crispy pastry filled with a spiced mixture of potatoes and peas. This air fryer version ensures a healthier alternative with the same delicious flavour and crunch.

Serves: 4 | Difficulty: Moderate | Prep Time: 30 minutes | Cook Time: 15 minutes | Total Time: 45 minutes

INGREDIENT LIST:

For the Pastry:
- 200g plain flour
- 1/2 tsp salt
- 2 tbsp vegetable oil
- 100ml water (or as needed)

For the Filling:
- 3 medium potatoes, boiled and diced
- 100g frozen peas, thawed
- 1 small onion, finely chopped
- 2 cloves garlic, minced
- 1 tsp grated ginger
- 1 tsp cumin seeds
- 1 tsp garam masala
- 1/2 tsp ground coriander
- 1/2 tsp ground turmeric
- 1/2 tsp chilli powder
- 2 tbsp vegetable oil
- Salt, to taste
- Fresh coriander, chopped, for garnish

PREPARATION:

1. **Make the Pastry:** In a large bowl, combine the plain flour and salt. Add the vegetable oil and rub it into the flour until the mixture resembles breadcrumbs. Gradually add water, mixing until a smooth dough forms. Cover and let it rest for 20 minutes.
2. **Prepare the Filling:** In a pan, heat 2 tbsp of vegetable oil over medium heat. Add the cumin seeds and let them sizzle for a few seconds. Add the chopped onion, minced garlic, and grated ginger, and sauté until the onion is soft. Add the diced potatoes, peas, garam masala, ground coriander, ground turmeric, chilli powder, and salt. Cook for 5-7 minutes, stirring occasionally. Remove from heat and let the mixture cool slightly. Stir in the chopped fresh coriander.
3. **Assemble the Samosas:** Divide the dough into 8 equal portions and roll each portion into a ball. Roll each ball into a thin oval shape. Cut each oval in half to form two semi-circles. Brush the straight edge of each semi-circle with water, fold it into a cone shape, and press the edges to seal. Fill the cone with the potato mixture and pinch the top edges to seal the samosa. Repeat with the remaining dough and filling.
4. **Preheat the Air Fryer:** Preheat the air fryer to 180 °C (360 °F).
5. **Air Fry the Samosas:** Lightly brush the samosas with vegetable oil. Place them in the air fryer basket in a single layer, ensuring they do not touch. Cook for 12-15 minutes, turning halfway through, until the samosas are golden brown and crispy.
6. **Serve:** Transfer the samosas to a serving plate and serve hot with mint chutney or tamarind sauce.

Tip: For extra flavour, you can add a handful of chopped fresh mint to the filling mixture. Ensure the samosas are sealed well to prevent the filling from spilling out during cooking.

ESTIMATED NUTRITIONAL TABLE PER 100G:
Calories: approx 180 kcal | Fat: approx 7 g | Carbohydrates: approx 25 g | Fibre: approx 3 g | Protein: approx 4 g | Salt: approx 0.6 g

BUTTER CHICKEN

Butter Chicken, or Murgh Makhani, is a beloved Indian dish featuring tender chicken pieces in a rich and creamy tomato-based sauce. This air fryer version ensures perfectly cooked chicken with a luscious, flavourful sauce.

Serves: 4 | Difficulty: Moderate | Prep Time: 20 minutes (plus marinating time) | Cook Time: 25 minutes | Total Time: 45 minutes (plus marinating time)

INGREDIENT LIST:

For the Chicken Marinade:
- 500g chicken breast or thighs, cut into bite-sized pieces
- 150g plain yoghurt
- 1 tbsp lemon juice
- 2 cloves garlic, minced
- 1 tsp grated ginger
- 1 tsp ground cumin
- 1 tsp ground coriander
- 1 tsp turmeric powder
- 1 tsp chilli powder
- 1/2 tsp salt

For the Sauce:
- 2 tbsp butter
- 1 large onion, finely chopped
- 3 cloves garlic, minced
- 1 tsp grated ginger
- 1 tsp ground cumin
- 1 tsp ground coriander
- 1 tsp garam masala
- 1/2 tsp turmeric powder
- 1/2 tsp chilli powder
- 400g canned chopped tomatoes
- 200ml double cream
- 1 tbsp tomato paste
- Salt and pepper, to taste
- Fresh coriander, chopped, for garnish

PREPARATION:

1. **Marinate the Chicken:** In a large bowl, mix the plain yoghurt, lemon juice, minced garlic, grated ginger, ground cumin, ground coriander, turmeric powder, chilli powder, and salt. Add the chicken pieces and mix until well coated. Cover and refrigerate for at least 1 hour, or overnight for best results.
2. **Preheat the Air Fryer:** Preheat the air fryer to 200 °C (390 °F).
3. **Cook the Chicken:** Place the marinated chicken pieces in the air fryer basket in a single layer. Cook for 10-12 minutes, turning halfway through, until the chicken is cooked through and slightly charred. Remove and set aside.
4. **Prepare the Sauce:** In a large pan, melt the butter over medium heat. Add the finely chopped onion, minced garlic, and grated ginger, and cook until the onion is soft and translucent. Add the ground cumin, ground coriander, garam masala, turmeric powder, and chilli powder. Cook for another 2 minutes, stirring frequently.
5. **Add the Tomatoes and Cream:** Stir in the chopped tomatoes and tomato paste, and simmer for 10 minutes until the sauce thickens. Reduce the heat to low, then stir in the double cream. Season with salt and pepper to taste.
6. **Combine Chicken and Sauce:** Add the cooked chicken pieces to the sauce and simmer for another 5 minutes, allowing the flavours to meld together.
7. **Serve:** Garnish with chopped fresh coriander and serve hot with naan bread or steamed rice.

Tip: For an extra layer of flavour, you can add a teaspoon of fenugreek leaves (kasuri methi) to the sauce. Make sure to use full-fat yoghurt in the marinade to keep the chicken tender and juicy.

ESTIMATED NUTRITIONAL TABLE PER 100G:
Calories: approx 220 kcal | Fat: approx 14 g | Carbohydrates: approx 6 g | Fibre: approx 1 g | Protein: approx 18 g | Salt: approx 0.7 g

NAAN BREAD

Naan Bread is a popular Indian flatbread known for its soft, fluffy texture and slightly chewy bite. This air fryer version ensures a quick and easy way to make perfect naan bread at home.

Serves: 4 | Difficulty: Easy | Prep Time: 15 minutes (plus rising time) | Cook Time: 10 minutes | Total Time: 25 minutes (plus rising time)

INGREDIENT LIST:

- 250g plain flour
- 1 tsp sugar
- 1 tsp salt
- 1 tsp instant yeast
- 2 tbsp plain yoghurt
- 2 tbsp vegetable oil
- 120ml warm water
- 2 cloves garlic, minced (optional)
- 2 tbsp melted butter or ghee
- Fresh coriander, chopped, for garnish

PREPARATION:

1. **Make the Dough:** In a large bowl, combine the plain flour, sugar, salt, and instant yeast. Add the plain yoghurt, vegetable oil, and warm water. Mix until a soft dough forms. Knead the dough on a floured surface for about 5 minutes until smooth and elastic.
2. **Let the Dough Rise:** Place the dough in a greased bowl, cover with a damp cloth, and let it rise in a warm place for about 1 hour, or until doubled in size.
3. **Preheat the Air Fryer:** Preheat the air fryer to 180 °C (360 °F).
4. **Shape the Naan:** Divide the dough into 4 equal portions. Roll each portion into a ball and flatten it into an oval or round shape about 1/4-inch thick. If using, press the minced garlic into the surface of the dough.
5. **Air Fry the Naan:** Lightly brush the air fryer basket with melted butter or ghee. Place the naan in the basket in a single layer, ensuring they do not touch. Cook for 3-4 minutes on each side, or until the naan is puffed and golden brown.
6. **Serve:** Brush the cooked naan with more melted butter or ghee and sprinkle with chopped fresh coriander. Serve hot.

Tip: For extra flavour, you can add a teaspoon of nigella seeds or sesame seeds to the dough before rolling it out. Naan bread is best enjoyed fresh but can be reheated in the air fryer for a few minutes if needed.

ESTIMATED NUTRITIONAL TABLE PER 100G:

Calories: approx 250 kcal | Fat: approx 8 g | Carbohydrates: approx 38 g | Fibre: approx 2 g | Protein: approx 5 g | Salt: approx 0.6 g

GULAB JAMUN

Gulab Jamun is a traditional Indian dessert made of deep-fried dough balls soaked in a sweet, fragrant syrup. This air fryer version provides a healthier alternative while maintaining the delicious taste and texture.

Serves: 4 | Difficulty: Moderate | Prep Time: 20 minutes | Cook Time: 15 minutes | Total Time: 35 minutes (plus soaking time)

INGREDIENT LIST:

For the Dough Balls:
- 100g milk powder
- 30g plain flour
- 1/2 tsp baking powder
- 1 tbsp ghee (clarified butter)
- 2-3 tbsp milk (as needed to form the dough)
- 1/4 tsp cardamom powder

For the Syrup:
- 200g granulated sugar
- 250ml water
- 1 tsp rose water (optional)
- 1/2 tsp cardamom powder
- A few saffron strands (optional)

PREPARATION:

1. **Make the Dough Balls:** In a bowl, combine the milk powder, plain flour, baking powder, and cardamom powder. Add the ghee and mix until the mixture resembles breadcrumbs. Gradually add milk, one tablespoon at a time, until a soft dough forms. Knead gently for a few minutes until smooth. Divide the dough into small, equal-sized balls (about 12-15).
2. **Preheat the Air Fryer:** Preheat the air fryer to 180 °C (360 °F).
3. **Air Fry the Dough Balls:** Lightly brush or spray the dough balls with a small amount of oil. Place them in the air fryer basket in a single layer. Cook for 10-12 minutes, turning halfway through, until the balls are golden brown and cooked through.
4. **Prepare the Syrup:** While the dough balls are cooking, prepare the syrup. In a saucepan, combine the granulated sugar and water. Bring to a boil over medium heat, stirring until the sugar dissolves. Add the rose water, cardamom powder, and saffron strands, if using. Reduce the heat and let it simmer for 5 minutes.
5. **Soak the Dough Balls:** Once the dough balls are cooked, remove them from the air fryer and let them cool slightly. Place the warm dough balls into the hot syrup, ensuring they are fully submerged. Let them soak for at least 1 hour to absorb the syrup.
6. **Serve:** Serve the Gulab Jamun warm or at room temperature, garnished with a few saffron strands or chopped nuts if desired.

Tip: For an extra rich flavour, you can use evaporated milk instead of regular milk in the dough. Ensure the dough balls are evenly sized to ensure uniform cooking.

ESTIMATED NUTRITIONAL TABLE PER 100G:
Calories: approx 250 kcal | Fat: approx 8 g | Carbohydrates: approx 40 g | Fibre: approx 1 g | Protein: approx 4 g | Salt: approx 0.2 g

THAILAND

SATAY SKEWERS

Satay Skewers are a popular Thai dish featuring marinated meat grilled on skewers and served with a delicious peanut sauce. This air fryer version ensures the meat is tender and flavourful with a perfect char.

Serves: 4 | Difficulty: Easy | Prep Time: 15 minutes (plus marinating time) | Cook Time: 10 minutes | Total Time: 25 minutes (plus marinating time)

INGREDIENT LIST:
For the Satay Marinade:
- 500g chicken breast or thigh, cut into bite-sized pieces
- 2 cloves garlic, minced
- 1 tbsp grated ginger
- 2 tbsp soy sauce
- 2 tbsp fish sauce
- 2 tbsp lime juice
- 1 tbsp brown sugar
- 1 tsp ground coriander
- 1 tsp ground turmeric
- 1 tbsp vegetable oil
- Wooden skewers, soaked in water for 30 minutes

For the Peanut Sauce:
- 100g smooth peanut butter
- 200ml coconut milk
- 1 tbsp soy sauce
- 1 tbsp fish sauce
- 1 tbsp lime juice
- 1 tbsp brown sugar
- 1 clove garlic, minced
- 1 tsp grated ginger
- 1/2 tsp chilli flakes (optional)

PREPARATION:
1. **Marinate the Chicken:** In a large bowl, combine the minced garlic, grated ginger, soy sauce, fish sauce, lime juice, brown sugar, ground coriander, ground turmeric, and vegetable oil. Add the chicken pieces and mix until well coated. Cover and refrigerate for at least 1 hour, or overnight for best results.
2. **Prepare the Peanut Sauce:** In a small saucepan, combine the peanut butter, coconut milk, soy sauce, fish sauce, lime juice, brown sugar, minced garlic, grated ginger, and chilli flakes (if using). Cook over medium heat, stirring constantly, until the sauce is smooth and slightly thickened. Remove from heat and set aside.
3. **Preheat the Air Fryer:** Preheat the air fryer to 200 °C (390 °F).
4. **Assemble the Skewers:** Thread the marinated chicken pieces onto the soaked wooden skewers.
5. **Cook the Skewers:** Place the skewers in the air fryer basket in a single layer. Cook for 8-10 minutes, turning halfway through, until the chicken is cooked through and slightly charred.
6. **Serve:** Transfer the satay skewers to a serving plate and serve hot with the peanut sauce on the side.

Tip: For extra flavour, you can garnish the satay skewers with chopped fresh coriander and crushed peanuts. Serve with a side of cucumber salad for a refreshing accompaniment.

ESTIMATED NUTRITIONAL TABLE PER 100G:
Calories: approx 250 kcal | Fat: approx 16 g | Carbohydrates: approx 8 g | Fibre: approx 1 g | Protein: approx 20 g | Salt: approx 1.2 g

PAD THAI

Pad Thai is a classic Thai street food dish featuring stir-fried rice noodles with shrimp, tofu, or chicken, combined with a tangy, sweet, and savoury sauce. This air fryer version ensures a quick and easy way to enjoy this delicious dish at home.

Serves: 4 | Difficulty: Moderate | Prep Time: 15 minutes | Cook Time: 15 minutes | Total Time: 30 minutes

INGREDIENT LIST:

- 200g rice noodles
- 200g shrimp, peeled and deveined (or chicken breast, thinly sliced)
- 100g firm tofu, cubed
- 2 tbsp vegetable oil
- 2 eggs, beaten
- 3 cloves garlic, minced
- 1 red bell pepper, thinly sliced
- 100g bean sprouts
- 3 spring onions, sliced
- 50g crushed peanuts
- Fresh coriander, chopped, for garnish
- Lime wedges, for serving

For the Pad Thai Sauce:
- 3 tbsp fish sauce
- 3 tbsp tamarind paste
- 2 tbsp brown sugar
- 1 tbsp soy sauce
- 1 tsp chilli flakes (optional)

PREPARATION:

1. **Prepare the Noodles:** Cook the rice noodles according to the package instructions until al dente. Drain and set aside.
2. **Make the Pad Thai Sauce:** In a small bowl, whisk together the fish sauce, tamarind paste, brown sugar, soy sauce, and chilli flakes (if using). Set aside.
3. **Preheat the Air Fryer:** Preheat the air fryer to 180 °C (360 °F).
4. **Cook the Tofu and Shrimp:** In an air fryer-safe pan or dish, add 1 tbsp of vegetable oil. Add the cubed tofu and shrimp (or chicken) to the pan. Cook in the air fryer for 5-7 minutes, shaking the pan halfway through, until the shrimp is pink and cooked through, and the tofu is golden. Remove and set aside.
5. **Cook the Vegetables:** Add the remaining 1 tbsp of vegetable oil to the pan. Add the minced garlic and sliced red bell pepper. Cook in the air fryer for 3-4 minutes until the vegetables are tender.
6. **Combine Ingredients:** Add the cooked rice noodles, tofu, shrimp, beaten eggs, bean sprouts, and spring onions to the pan with the vegetables. Pour the Pad Thai sauce over the top. Toss everything together to combine well. Cook in the air fryer for an additional 3-5 minutes until everything is heated through and the eggs are cooked.
7. **Serve:** Transfer the Pad Thai to a serving dish. Garnish with crushed peanuts, chopped fresh coriander, and lime wedges. Serve hot.

Tip: For added flavour, you can garnish the Pad Thai with additional chilli flakes or a drizzle of sriracha sauce. Ensure the rice noodles are not overcooked to maintain their texture in the final dish.

ESTIMATED NUTRITIONAL TABLE PER 100G:
Calories: approx 200 kcal | Fat: approx 10 g | Carbohydrates: approx 20 g | Fibre: approx 2 g | Protein: approx 10 g | Salt: approx 1.0 g

THAI BASIL VEGETABLES

Thai Basil Vegetables is a vibrant and flavourful dish featuring a mix of vegetables stir-fried with fragrant Thai basil and a savoury sauce. This air fryer version ensures the vegetables retain their crisp texture and fresh flavours.

Serves: 4 | Difficulty: Easy | Prep Time: 15 minutes | Cook Time: 10 minutes | Total Time: 25 minutes

INGREDIENT LIST:

- 1 red bell pepper, sliced
- 1 yellow bell pepper, sliced
- 1 courgette, sliced
- 100g green beans, trimmed
- 1 onion, sliced
- 2 cloves garlic, minced
- 1 tbsp vegetable oil
- 50g Thai basil leaves
- 1 red chilli, sliced (optional)
- Cooked jasmine rice, for serving

For the Sauce:
- 2 tbsp soy sauce
- 1 tbsp oyster sauce
- 1 tbsp fish sauce
- 1 tbsp brown sugar
- 1 tbsp water

PREPARATION:

1. **Prepare the Sauce:** In a small bowl, whisk together the soy sauce, oyster sauce, fish sauce, brown sugar, and water. Set aside.
2. **Preheat the Air Fryer:** Preheat the air fryer to 180 °C (360 °F).
3. **Cook the Vegetables:** In an air fryer-safe pan or dish, add the vegetable oil, sliced red and yellow bell peppers, courgette, green beans, and onion. Cook in the air fryer for 8-10 minutes, shaking the pan halfway through, until the vegetables are tender but still crisp.
4. **Add the Garlic and Chilli:** Add the minced garlic and sliced red chilli (if using) to the pan with the vegetables. Cook for an additional 2 minutes.
5. **Combine with Sauce and Basil:** Pour the sauce over the vegetables and toss to coat evenly. Add the Thai basil leaves and cook for another 2 minutes, until the basil is wilted and fragrant.
6. **Serve:** Transfer the Thai Basil Vegetables to a serving dish and serve hot with cooked jasmine rice.

Tip: For added protein, you can include tofu, chicken, or shrimp in the dish. Ensure the Thai basil is added at the end to preserve its delicate flavour and aroma.

ESTIMATED NUTRITIONAL TABLE PER 100G:
Calories: approx 90 kcal | Fat: approx 4 g | Carbohydrates: approx 10 g | Fibre: approx 2 g | Protein: approx 2 g | Salt: approx 0.8 g

MANGO STICKY RICE

Mango Sticky Rice is a beloved Thai dessert featuring sweet sticky rice paired with ripe mango slices and drizzled with a rich coconut sauce. This air fryer version ensures a perfectly cooked sticky rice and a delightful tropical flavour.

Serves: 4 | Difficulty: Moderate | Prep Time: 20 minutes (plus soaking time) | Cook Time: 25 minutes | Total Time: 45 minutes (plus soaking time)

INGREDIENT LIST:

- 200g glutinous rice
- 400ml coconut milk
- 100g granulated sugar
- 1/2 tsp salt
- 2 ripe mangoes, peeled and sliced
- 1 tbsp toasted sesame seeds (optional)
- Fresh mint leaves, for garnish

PREPARATION:

1. **Soak the Rice:** Rinse the glutinous rice under cold water until the water runs clear. Soak the rice in water for at least 1 hour, or overnight for best results. Drain well.
2. **Preheat the Air Fryer:** Preheat the air fryer to 180 °C (360 °F).
3. **Cook the Rice:** Place the soaked and drained rice in an air fryer-safe dish. Add 200ml of coconut milk, 50g of granulated sugar, and 1/4 tsp of salt. Mix well. Cover the dish with aluminium foil and cook in the air fryer for 20-25 minutes, stirring halfway through, until the rice is tender and all the liquid is absorbed.
4. **Prepare the Coconut Sauce:** In a small saucepan, combine the remaining 200ml of coconut milk, 50g of granulated sugar, and 1/4 tsp of salt. Cook over medium heat, stirring constantly, until the sugar is dissolved and the sauce is slightly thickened. Remove from heat and let it cool slightly.
5. **Serve:** Divide the sticky rice among serving plates. Arrange the sliced mangoes on the side. Drizzle the coconut sauce over the rice and sprinkle with toasted sesame seeds if using. Garnish with fresh mint leaves.

Tip: For added flavour, you can infuse the coconut milk with a pandan leaf while cooking the rice. Ensure the mangoes are ripe and sweet for the best taste.

ESTIMATED NUTRITIONAL TABLE PER 100G:

Calories: approx 200 kcal | Fat: approx 8 g | Carbohydrates: approx 30 g | Fibre: approx 1 g | Protein: approx 2 g | Salt: approx 0.2 g

CHAPTER 5: MIDDLE EAST

LEBANON

FALAFEL

Falafel is a popular Middle Eastern dish made from ground chickpeas, herbs, and spices, formed into balls or patties and fried until crispy. This air fryer version offers a healthier take on the traditional falafel while maintaining its delicious flavour and texture.

Serves: 4 | Difficulty: Moderate | Prep Time: 20 minutes (plus soaking time) |
Cook Time: 15 minutes | Total Time: 35 minutes (plus soaking time)

INGREDIENT LIST:

- 200g dried chickpeas
- 1 small onion, finely chopped
- 3 cloves garlic, minced
- 1 bunch fresh parsley, chopped
- 1 bunch fresh coriander, chopped
- 1 tsp ground cumin
- 1 tsp ground coriander
- 1 tsp salt
- 1/2 tsp black pepper
- 1/2 tsp baking powder
- 2 tbsp plain flour
- 2 tbsp olive oil (for brushing)
- Lemon wedges, for serving
- Tahini sauce, for serving

PREPARATION:

1. **Soak the Chickpeas:** Rinse the dried chickpeas and place them in a large bowl. Cover with plenty of cold water and let them soak overnight or for at least 12 hours. Drain and rinse well.
2. **Make the Falafel Mixture:** In a food processor, combine the soaked chickpeas, chopped onion, minced garlic, fresh parsley, fresh coriander, ground cumin, ground coriander, salt, black pepper, and baking powder. Pulse until the mixture is finely ground but not pureed. Transfer the mixture to a bowl and stir in the plain flour.
3. **Form the Falafel Balls:** Using your hands, shape the falafel mixture into small balls or patties, about the size of a walnut. Place them on a baking tray.
4. **Preheat the Air Fryer:** Preheat the air fryer to 180 °C (360 °F).
5. **Air Fry the Falafel:** Lightly brush the falafel balls with olive oil. Place them in the air fryer basket in a single layer, ensuring they do not touch. Cook for 12-15 minutes, turning halfway through, until the falafel are golden brown and crispy.
6. **Serve:** Transfer the falafel to a serving plate and serve hot with lemon wedges and tahini sauce.

Tip: For extra flavour, you can add a pinch of chilli flakes or a dash of ground turmeric to the falafel mixture. Serve the falafel in pita bread with fresh vegetables and a drizzle of tahini sauce for a complete meal.

ESTIMATED NUTRITIONAL TABLE PER 100G:
Calories: approx 180 kcal | Fat: approx 8 g | Carbohydrates: approx 22 g |
Fibre: approx 6 g | Protein: approx 6 g | Salt: approx 0.8 g

SHAWARMA

Shawarma is a popular Middle Eastern dish featuring marinated meat that's typically cooked on a vertical rotisserie. This air fryer version ensures tender, flavourful chicken with a deliciously charred exterior.

Serves: 4 | Difficulty: Moderate | Prep Time: 20 minutes (plus marinating time) | Cook Time: 25 minutes | Total Time: 45 minutes (plus marinating time)

INGREDIENT LIST:

- 500g chicken thighs, boneless and skinless
- 3 tbsp olive oil
- 1 tbsp lemon juice
- 3 cloves garlic, minced
- 1 tsp ground cumin
- 1 tsp ground coriander
- 1 tsp ground paprika
- 1/2 tsp ground turmeric
- 1/2 tsp ground cinnamon
- 1/2 tsp ground allspice
- 1/2 tsp ground black pepper
- 1/2 tsp salt
- 1/4 tsp cayenne pepper (optional)
- 4 pita breads
- Fresh vegetables (tomato, cucumber, red onion), sliced
- Tahini sauce or garlic sauce, for serving

PREPARATION:

1. **Marinate the Chicken:** In a large bowl, combine the olive oil, lemon juice, minced garlic, ground cumin, ground coriander, ground paprika, ground turmeric, ground cinnamon, ground allspice, ground black pepper, salt, and cayenne pepper (if using). Add the chicken thighs and mix well to coat. Cover and marinate in the refrigerator for at least 1 hour, or overnight for best results.
2. **Preheat the Air Fryer:** Preheat the air fryer to 200 °C (390 °F).
3. **Cook the Chicken:** Place the marinated chicken thighs in the air fryer basket in a single layer. Cook for 20-25 minutes, turning halfway through, until the chicken is cooked through and slightly charred on the edges. Remove from the air fryer and let rest for a few minutes.
4. **Slice the Chicken:** Thinly slice the cooked chicken thighs into strips.
5. **Assemble the Shawarma:** Warm the pita breads in the air fryer for a few minutes if desired. Fill each pita with the sliced chicken, fresh vegetables, and a drizzle of tahini sauce or garlic sauce.
6. **Serve:** Serve the shawarma hot, with extra sauce on the side if desired.

Tip: For added flavour, you can add a sprinkle of sumac or a few fresh mint leaves to the shawarma. Serve with a side of pickles and hummus for a complete meal.

ESTIMATED NUTRITIONAL TABLE PER 100G:

Calories: approx 200 kcal | Fat: approx 10 g | Carbohydrates: approx 15 g | Fibre: approx 2 g | Protein: approx 15 g | Salt: approx 0.7 g

HUMMUS AND PITA CHIPS

Hummus and Pita Chips is a classic Middle Eastern snack featuring creamy chickpea dip served with crispy, seasoned pita chips. This air fryer version ensures perfectly golden pita chips with a delicious crunch.

Serves: 4 | Difficulty: Easy | Prep Time: 10 minutes | Cook Time: 10 minutes | Total Time: 20 minutes

INGREDIENT LIST:

For the Hummus:
- 400g canned chickpeas, drained and rinsed
- 2 cloves garlic, minced
- 3 tbsp tahini
- 3 tbsp olive oil
- 3 tbsp lemon juice
- 1 tsp ground cumin
- Salt, to taste
- Water, as needed

For the Pita Chips:
- 4 pita breads
- 2 tbsp olive oil
- 1 tsp garlic powder
- 1 tsp ground paprika
- 1/2 tsp salt

PREPARATION:

1. **Make the Hummus:** In a food processor, combine the chickpeas, minced garlic, tahini, olive oil, lemon juice, ground cumin, and salt. Blend until smooth, adding water a tablespoon at a time until the desired consistency is reached. Adjust seasoning to taste. Transfer to a serving bowl and drizzle with extra olive oil if desired.
2. **Preheat the Air Fryer:** Preheat the air fryer to 180 °C (360 °F).
3. **Prepare the Pita Chips:** Cut each pita bread into 8 wedges and place them in a large bowl. Drizzle with olive oil and sprinkle with garlic powder, ground paprika, and salt. Toss to coat the pita wedges evenly.
4. **Air Fry the Pita Chips:** Place the seasoned pita wedges in the air fryer basket in a single layer. Cook for 5-7 minutes, shaking the basket halfway through, until the pita chips are golden and crispy. You may need to cook them in batches depending on the size of your air fryer.
5. **Serve:** Transfer the pita chips to a serving plate and serve alongside the hummus.

Tip: For extra flavour, you can sprinkle the pita chips with a pinch of dried oregano or za'atar seasoning before air frying. The hummus can be garnished with a sprinkle of paprika, chopped fresh parsley, or a few whole chickpeas.

ESTIMATED NUTRITIONAL TABLE PER 100G:
Calories: approx 250 kcal | Fat: approx 12 g | Carbohydrates: approx 28 g | Fibre: approx 6 g | Protein: approx 7 g | Salt: approx 0.8 g

BAKLAVA

Baklava is a rich and sweet Middle Eastern dessert made with layers of phyllo pastry, filled with chopped nuts, and soaked in a fragrant honey syrup. This air fryer version ensures a perfectly crispy and delicious baklava.

Serves: 8 | Difficulty: Moderate | Prep Time: 30 minutes | Cook Time: 20 minutes | Total Time: 50 minutes

INGREDIENT LIST:

For the Baklava:
- 200g phyllo pastry sheets
- 150g unsalted butter, melted
- 200g mixed nuts (walnuts, pistachios, almonds), finely chopped
- 1 tsp ground cinnamon
- 1/4 tsp ground cloves

For the Syrup:
- 200g granulated sugar
- 120ml water
- 120ml honey
- 1 tbsp lemon juice
- 1 tsp vanilla extract
- 1 cinnamon stick

PREPARATION:

1. **Prepare the Nut Filling:** In a bowl, combine the finely chopped mixed nuts, ground cinnamon, and ground cloves. Set aside.
2. **Assemble the Baklava:** Preheat the air fryer to 160 °C (320 °F). Brush an air fryer-safe baking dish with melted butter. Place one sheet of phyllo pastry in the dish and brush with melted butter. Repeat, layering and buttering, until you have about 5 sheets layered.
3. **Add the Nut Filling:** Sprinkle a thin layer of the nut mixture over the phyllo. Continue layering with 3 more phyllo sheets, brushing each with butter, then sprinkle with another layer of nuts. Repeat until all the nuts are used, finishing with a top layer of about 5 phyllo sheets.
4. **Cut the Baklava:** Using a sharp knife, cut the baklava into diamond or square shapes.
5. **Air Fry the Baklava:** Place the assembled baklava in the air fryer basket and cook for 15-20 minutes, or until the phyllo is golden brown and crispy.
6. **Prepare the Syrup:** While the baklava is cooking, make the syrup. In a saucepan, combine the granulated sugar, water, honey, lemon juice, vanilla extract, and cinnamon stick. Bring to a boil over medium heat, then reduce the heat and simmer for 10 minutes. Remove from heat and let cool slightly.
7. **Soak the Baklava:** Remove the baklava from the air fryer and immediately pour the warm syrup over it, ensuring it gets into all the cuts and layers. Let the baklava cool completely to absorb the syrup.
8. **Serve:** Once the baklava is cool, transfer it to a serving plate. Serve at room temperature.

Tip: For added flavour, you can sprinkle some finely chopped pistachios over the top before serving. Baklava can be stored in an airtight container at room temperature for up to a week.

ESTIMATED NUTRITIONAL TABLE PER 100G:
Calories: approx 300 kcal | Fat: approx 20 g | Carbohydrates: approx 30 g | Fibre: approx 2 g | Protein: approx 4 g | Salt: approx 0.1 g

TURKEY

SIGARA BOREK (CHEESE ROLLS)

Sigara Börek are Turkish cheese-filled pastries made from thin phyllo dough, rolled into a cigar shape, and fried until crispy. This air fryer version provides a healthier alternative while ensuring a perfect, crunchy texture.

Serves: 4 | Difficulty: Easy | Prep Time: 15 minutes | Cook Time: 12 minutes | Total Time: 27 minutes

INGREDIENT LIST:

- 200g feta cheese, crumbled
- 100g ricotta cheese
- 2 tbsp fresh parsley, finely chopped
- 1 egg, beaten
- 1/4 tsp black pepper
- 12 sheets of phyllo pastry
- 50g melted butter or vegetable oil (for brushing)

PREPARATION:

1. **Prepare the Filling:** In a bowl, combine the crumbled feta cheese, ricotta cheese, chopped parsley, beaten egg, and black pepper. Mix until well combined.
2. **Assemble the Börek:** Preheat the air fryer to 180 °C (360 °F). Lay a sheet of phyllo pastry on a clean surface and brush lightly with melted butter or vegetable oil. Place a spoonful of the cheese mixture at one end of the phyllo sheet. Fold in the sides and roll up tightly into a cigar shape. Repeat with the remaining sheets and filling.
3. **Air Fry the Börek:** Place the rolled börek in the air fryer basket in a single layer, ensuring they do not touch. Lightly brush the tops with more melted butter or oil. Cook for 10-12 minutes, turning halfway through, until golden brown and crispy.
4. **Serve:** Transfer the börek to a serving plate and serve hot.

Tip: For a variation, you can add a pinch of red pepper flakes to the cheese filling for a bit of heat. Serve with a side of yoghurt or a simple cucumber and tomato salad.

ESTIMATED NUTRITIONAL TABLE PER 100G:

Calories: approx 250 kcal | Fat: approx 15 g | Carbohydrates: approx 20 g | Fibre: approx 1 g | Protein: approx 8 g | Salt: approx 1.0 g

DONER KEBAB

Doner Kebab is a popular Turkish dish featuring spiced meat cooked on a vertical rotisserie and thinly sliced. This air fryer version allows you to achieve tender, flavourful meat with a deliciously charred exterior.

Serves: 4 | Difficulty: Moderate | Prep Time: 20 minutes (plus marinating time) | Cook Time: 30 minutes | Total Time: 50 minutes (plus marinating time)

INGREDIENT LIST:

- 500g lamb or beef, thinly sliced
- 1 large onion, grated
- 3 cloves garlic, minced
- 3 tbsp plain yoghurt
- 2 tbsp olive oil
- 1 tbsp lemon juice
- 1 tbsp tomato paste
- 2 tsp ground cumin
- 2 tsp ground coriander
- 2 tsp ground paprika
- 1 tsp ground cinnamon
- 1 tsp ground black pepper
- 1 tsp salt
- 1/2 tsp ground allspice
- Pita bread, for serving
- Fresh vegetables (tomato, cucumber, red onion), sliced
- Garlic sauce or tahini sauce, for serving

PREPARATION:

1. **Marinate the Meat:** In a large bowl, combine the grated onion, minced garlic, plain yoghurt, olive oil, lemon juice, tomato paste, ground cumin, ground coriander, ground paprika, ground cinnamon, ground black pepper, salt, and ground allspice. Add the thinly sliced meat and mix well to coat. Cover and marinate in the refrigerator for at least 1 hour, or overnight for best results.
2. **Preheat the Air Fryer:** Preheat the air fryer to 200 °C (390 °F).
3. **Cook the Meat:** Arrange the marinated meat slices in the air fryer basket in a single layer. Cook for 25-30 minutes, shaking the basket halfway through, until the meat is cooked through and slightly charred on the edges.
4. **Assemble the Kebab:** Warm the pita bread in the air fryer for a few minutes if desired. Fill each pita with the cooked meat, fresh vegetables, and a drizzle of garlic sauce or tahini sauce.
5. **Serve:** Serve the doner kebabs hot, with extra sauce on the side if desired.

Tip: For an authentic touch, you can sprinkle the finished kebabs with a pinch of sumac or fresh parsley. Serve with a side of pickled vegetables and a simple salad for a complete meal.

ESTIMATED NUTRITIONAL TABLE PER 100G:

Calories: approx 250 kcal | Fat: approx 15 g | Carbohydrates: approx 5 g | Fibre: approx 1 g | Protein: approx 20 g | Salt: approx 0.8 g

BULGUR PILAF

Bulgur Pilaf is a traditional Turkish dish made with bulgur wheat, vegetables, and spices, creating a flavourful and nutritious side dish. This air fryer version ensures a quick and easy preparation while maintaining the authentic taste.

Serves: 4 | Difficulty: Easy | Prep Time: 10 minutes | Cook Time: 20 minutes | Total Time: 30 minutes

INGREDIENT LIST:

- 200g bulgur wheat
- 1 onion, finely chopped
- 1 red bell pepper, diced
- 2 cloves garlic, minced
- 2 tbsp olive oil
- 400ml chicken or vegetable stock
- 2 tomatoes, diced
- 1 tsp tomato paste
- 1 tsp ground cumin
- 1 tsp ground paprika
- Salt and pepper, to taste
- Fresh parsley, chopped, for garnish

PREPARATION:

1. **Preheat the Air Fryer:** Preheat the air fryer to 180 °C (360 °F).
2. **Cook the Vegetables:** In an air fryer-safe pan or dish, add the olive oil, chopped onion, diced red bell pepper, and minced garlic. Cook in the air fryer for 5 minutes until the vegetables are softened.
3. **Add the Bulgur and Spices:** Stir in the bulgur wheat, diced tomatoes, tomato paste, ground cumin, and ground paprika. Cook for an additional 2 minutes.
4. **Add the Stock:** Pour in the chicken or vegetable stock and season with salt and pepper. Stir to combine.
5. **Cook the Pilaf:** Cover the pan with aluminium foil and cook in the air fryer for 15 minutes, or until the bulgur is tender and has absorbed the liquid. Stir halfway through the cooking time to ensure even cooking.
6. **Serve:** Fluff the bulgur pilaf with a fork and transfer to a serving dish. Garnish with chopped fresh parsley and serve hot.

Tip: For added flavour, you can stir in some cooked chickpeas or toasted pine nuts before serving. Bulgur Pilaf pairs wonderfully with grilled meats, kebabs, or as part of a mezze spread.

ESTIMATED NUTRITIONAL TABLE PER 100G:
Calories: approx 120 kcal | Fat: approx 4 g | Carbohydrates: approx 20 g | Fibre: approx 3 g | Protein: approx 3 g | Salt: approx 0.5 g

LOKMA (SWEET FRIED DOUGH)

Lokma is a traditional Turkish dessert consisting of small dough balls that are deep-fried until golden and crispy, then soaked in a sweet syrup. This air fryer version provides a healthier alternative while retaining the delicious sweetness and texture.

Serves: 4 | Difficulty: Moderate | Prep Time: 15 minutes (plus rising time) | Cook Time: 15 minutes | Total Time: 30 minutes (plus rising time)

INGREDIENT LIST:

For the Dough:
- 200g plain flour
- 1 tbsp sugar
- 1/2 tsp salt
- 1 tsp instant yeast
- 150ml warm water
- 1 tbsp olive oil

For the Syrup:
- 200g granulated sugar
- 150ml water
- 1 tbsp lemon juice
- 1 tsp rose water (optional)

For Frying:
- 2 tbsp vegetable oil (for brushing)

PREPARATION:

1. **Prepare the Dough:** In a large bowl, combine the plain flour, sugar, salt, and instant yeast. Add the warm water and olive oil, mixing until a soft dough forms. Knead the dough on a floured surface for about 5 minutes until smooth and elastic. Place the dough in a greased bowl, cover with a damp cloth, and let it rise in a warm place for about 1 hour, or until doubled in size.
2. **Prepare the Syrup:** While the dough is rising, make the syrup. In a saucepan, combine the granulated sugar, water, and lemon juice. Bring to a boil over medium heat, then reduce the heat and simmer for 10 minutes until slightly thickened. Remove from heat and stir in the rose water, if using. Let the syrup cool.
3. **Preheat the Air Fryer:** Preheat the air fryer to 180 °C (360 °F).
4. **Shape and Cook the Dough:** Punch down the risen dough and divide it into small, bite-sized balls. Lightly brush the air fryer basket with vegetable oil. Place the dough balls in the basket in a single layer, ensuring they do not touch. Lightly brush the tops with more vegetable oil. Cook for 10-12 minutes, turning halfway through, until the dough balls are golden brown and cooked through.
5. **Soak in Syrup:** While the lokma are still hot, transfer them to a large bowl and pour the cooled syrup over them. Let them soak for a few minutes, turning occasionally to ensure they are evenly coated with syrup.
6. **Serve:** Transfer the soaked lokma to a serving plate. Serve warm, optionally garnished with a sprinkle of cinnamon or chopped nuts.

Tip: For extra flavour, you can add a pinch of ground cardamom to the dough. Lokma is best enjoyed fresh, but you can store leftovers in an airtight container at room temperature for up to a day.

ESTIMATED NUTRITIONAL TABLE PER 100G:
Calories: approx 250 kcal | Fat: approx 5 g | Carbohydrates: approx 45 g | Fibre: approx 1 g | Protein: approx 4 g | Salt: approx 0.3 g

CONCLUSION

As we come to the end of our culinary journey through this Ninja Air Fryer Cookbook, we hope you feel inspired and empowered to explore the diverse and delicious world of global cuisine. This book has taken you on a gastronomic adventure across continents, introducing you to a variety of flavours and cooking techniques that are now easily accessible with your Ninja Air Fryer.

Cooking is not just about following recipes; it's about experimenting, being creative and making each dish your own. We encourage you to use this cookbook as a starting point. Feel free to tweak the recipes, substitute ingredients and add your own personal touch to each dish. The beauty of cooking lies in its endless possibilities and the joy it brings to both the cook and those who share the meal. Take the opportunity to try new dishes from different cultures and broaden your culinary horizons. Whether it's the spicy and vibrant flavours of Thailand, the hearty and comforting dishes of Europe or the rich and aromatic dishes of the Middle East, there's a world of taste waiting to be explored. Remember, the Ninja Air Fryer is a versatile tool that can help you create healthier versions of your favourite recipes without sacrificing flavour or texture. Have fun discovering new ways to use your air fryer and don't be afraid to experiment with ingredients and cooking methods.

We hope this cookbook has not only provided you with delicious recipes, but also inspired a love of cooking and exploring different cultures through food. Thank you for joining us on this journey. Happy cooking, bon appétit and happy frying! May your kitchen be filled with the flavours of the world.

DISCLAIMER

The information provided in „The Ninja Air Fryer Cookbook UK XXL: Super-Delicious & Amazing Air Fryer Recipes for Everyday Enjoyment" is for general informational purposes only. While we strive to ensure the accuracy and reliability of the content, all recipes, nutritional facts, and tips are based on the author's knowledge and research as of the publication date.

Nutritional Information:
The nutritional information provided for each recipe is estimated and may vary based on the specific ingredients and brands used. We recommend consulting a registered dietitian or nutritionist for precise nutritional advice tailored to your individual dietary needs.

Health and Safety:
Always use your Ninja Air Fryer according to the manufacturer's instructions and safety guidelines. Ensure that all ingredients are fresh and handled properly to avoid foodborne illnesses. If you have any food allergies, please verify the ingredients of each recipe and consult with a healthcare professional if necessary.

Results May Vary:
The outcome of the recipes may vary depending on several factors, including the make and model of your air fryer, ingredient quality, and cooking techniques. Practice and adjustments may be required to achieve the desired results.

Medical Advice:
This cookbook is not intended to provide medical advice, diagnosis, or treatment. Always seek the advice of your physician or other qualified health provider with any questions you may have regarding a medical condition or dietary changes.

By using this cookbook, you acknowledge and agree that the authors and publishers are not responsible for any adverse reactions, effects, or consequences resulting from the use of any recipes or suggestions herein.

Trademarks:
„Ninja" is a registered trademark of SharkNinja Operating LLC. This book is not affiliated with, authorized, endorsed, or sponsored by SharkNinja Operating LLC.

For any concerns or questions about the content of this cookbook, please contact the publisher directly.

EXCLUSIVE BONUS

40 Weight Loss Recipes

&

14 Days Meal Plan

Scan the QR-Code and receive the FREE download:

Printed in Great Britain
by Amazon